MW01592696

MERCY IN THE STORM

A STUDY ON THE BOOK OF JONAH

JOANNA KIMBREL

STUDY SUGGESTIONS

We believe that the Bible is true, trustworthy, and timeless and that it is vitally important for all believers. These study suggestions are intended to help you more effectively study Scripture as you seek to know and love God through His Word.

SUGGESTED STUDY TOOLS

- A Bible

- A double-spaced, printed copy of the Scripture passages that this study covers. You can use a website like *www.biblegateway.com* to copy the text of a passage and print out a double-spaced copy to be able to mark on easily

- A journal to write notes or prayers

- Pens, colored pencils, and highlighters

- A dictionary to look up unfamiliar words

HOW TO USE THIS STUDY

Begin your study time in prayer. Ask God to reveal Himself to you, to help you understand what you are reading, and to transform you with His Word (Psalm 119:18).

Before you read what is written in each day of the study itself, read the assigned passages of Scripture for that day. Use your double-spaced copy to circle, underline, highlight, draw arrows, and mark in any way you would like to help you dig deeper as you work through a passage.

Read the daily written content provided for the current study day.

Answer the questions that appear at the end of each study day.

The inductive method provides tools for deeper and more intentional Bible study. To study the Bible inductively, work through the steps below after reading background information on the book.

1 OBSERVATION & COMPREHENSION
Key question: What does the text say?

After reading the daily Scripture in its entirety at least once, begin working with smaller portions of the Scripture. Read a passage of Scripture repetitively, and then mark the following items in the text:

- Key or repeated words and ideas
- Key themes
- Transition words (Ex: therefore, but, because, if/then, likewise, etc.)
- Lists
- Comparisons and contrasts
- Commands
- Unfamiliar words (look these up in a dictionary)
- Questions you have about the text

2 INTERPRETATION
Key question: What does the text mean?

Once you have annotated the text, work through the following steps to help you interpret its meaning:

- Read the passage in other versions for a better understanding of the text.
- Read cross-references to help interpret Scripture with Scripture.
- Paraphrase or summarize the passage to check for understanding.
- Identify how the text reflects the metanarrative of Scripture, which is the story of creation, fall, redemption, and restoration.
- Read trustworthy commentaries if you need further insight into the meaning of the passage.

APPLICATION
Key Question: How should the truth of this passage change me?

Bible study is not merely an intellectual pursuit. The truths about God, ourselves, and the gospel that we discover in Scripture should produce transformation in our hearts and lives. Answer the following questions as you consider what you have learned in your study:

- What attributes of God's character are revealed in the passage?

    Consider places where the text directly states the character of God, as well as how His character is revealed through His words and actions.

- What do I learn about myself in light of who God is?

    Consider how you fall short of God's character, how the text reveals your sin nature, and what it says about your new identity in Christ.

- How should this truth change me?

    A passage of Scripture may contain direct commands telling us what to do or warnings about sins to avoid in order to help us grow in holiness. Other times our application flows out of seeing ourselves in light of God's character. As we pray and reflect on how God is calling us to change in light of His Word, we should be asking questions like, "How should I pray for God to change my heart?" and "What practical steps can I take toward cultivating habits of holiness?"

THE ATTRIBUTES OF GOD

ETERNAL

God has no beginning
and no end. He always
was, always is,
and always will be.

HAB. 1:12 / REV. 1:8 / IS. 41:4

FAITHFUL

God is incapable of
anything but fidelity.
He is loyally devoted to
His plan and purpose.

2 TIM. 2:13 / DEUT. 7:9
HEB. 10:23

GOOD

God is pure; there is no
defilement in Him.
He is unable to sin, and
all He does is good.

GEN. 1:31 / PS. 34:8 / PS. 107:1

GRACIOUS

God is kind, giving
us gifts and benefits
we do not deserve.

2 KINGS 13:23 / PS. 145:8
IS. 30:18

HOLY

God is undefiled and
unable to be in the presence
of defilement. He is
sacred and set-apart.

REV. 4:8 / LEV. 19:2 / HAB. 1:13

INCOMPREHENSIBLE & TRANSCENDENT

God is high above and beyond
human understanding. He is
unable to be fully known.

PS. 145:3 / IS. 55:8-9
ROM. 11:33-36

IMMUTABLE

God does not change.
He is the same yesterday,
today, and tomorrow.

1 SAM. 15:29 / ROM. 11:29
JAMES 1:17

INFINITE

God is limitless. He exhibits
all of His attributes perfectly
and boundlessly.

ROM. 11:33-36 / IS. 40:28
PS. 147:5

JEALOUS

God is desirous of receiving
the praise and affection
He rightly deserves.

EX. 20:5 / DEUT. 4:23-24
JOSH. 24:19

JUST

God governs in
perfect justice. He acts in
accordance with justice.
In Him, there is no
wrongdoing or dishonesty.

IS. 61:8 / DEUT. 32:4 / PS. 146:7-9

LOVING

God is eternally, enduringly,
steadfastly loving and
affectionate. He does not
forsake or betray His
covenant love.

JN. 3:16 / EPH. 2:4-5 / 1 JN. 4:16

MERCIFUL

God is compassionate,
withholding from us the
wrath that we deserve.

TITUS 3:5 / PS. 25:10
LAM. 3:22-23

OMNIPOTENT

God is all-powerful;
His strength is unlimited.

MAT. 19:26 / JOB 42:1-2
JER. 32:27

OMNIPRESENT

God is everywhere;
His presence is near
and permeating.

PROV. 15:3 / PS. 139:7-10
JER. 23:23-24

OMNISCIENT

God is all-knowing;
there is nothing
unknown to Him.

PS. 147:4 / I JN. 3:20
HEB. 4:13

PATIENT

God is long-suffering and
enduring. He gives ample
opportunity for people
to turn toward Him.

ROM. 2:4 / 2 PET. 3:9 / PS. 86:15

SELF-EXISTENT

God was not created
but exists by His
power alone.

PS. 90:1-2 / JN. 1:4 / JN. 5:26

SELF-SUFFICIENT

God has no needs and
depends on nothing, but
everything depends on God.

IS. 40:28-31 / ACTS 17:24-25
PHIL. 4:19

SOVEREIGN

God governs over all things;
He is in complete control.

COL. 1:17 / PS. 24:1-2
1 CHRON. 29:11-12

TRUTHFUL

God is our measurement
of what is fact. By Him
we are able to discern
true and false.

JN. 3:33 / ROM. 1:25 / JN. 14:6

WISE

God is infinitely
knowledgeable and is
judicious with His
knowledge.

IS. 46:9-10 / IS. 55:9 / PROV. 3:19

WRATHFUL

God stands in opposition to
all that is evil. He enacts
judgment according to
His holiness, righteousness,
and justice.

PS. 69:24 / JN. 3:36 / ROM. 1:18

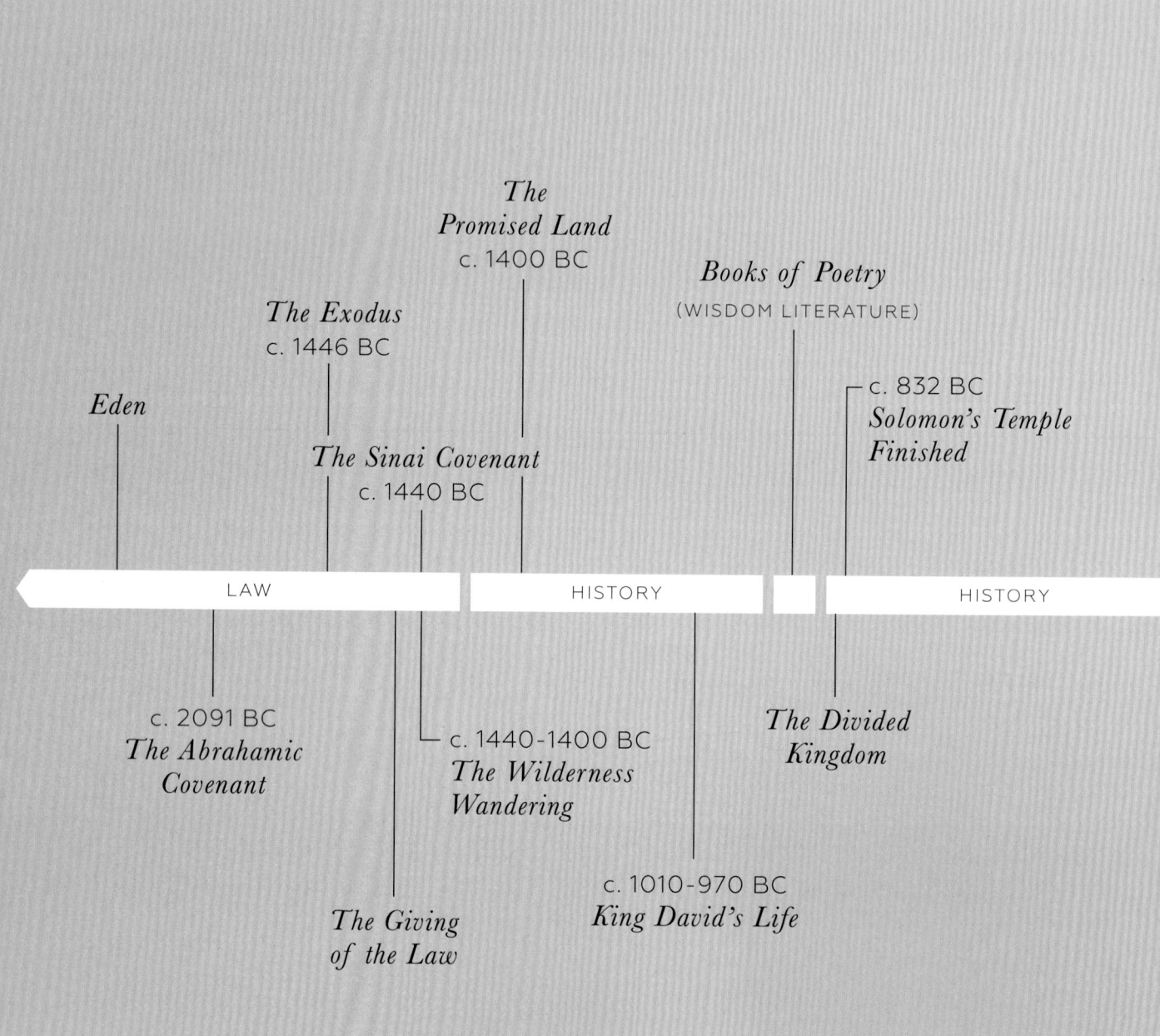

The
Promised Land
c. 1400 BC

Books of Poetry
(WISDOM LITERATURE)

The Exodus
c. 1446 BC

Eden

c. 832 BC
Solomon's Temple
Finished

The Sinai Covenant
c. 1440 BC

LAW   HISTORY   HISTORY

c. 2091 BC
The Abrahamic
Covenant

c. 1440-1400 BC
The Wilderness
Wandering

The Divided
Kingdom

c. 1010-970 BC
King David's Life

The Giving
of the Law

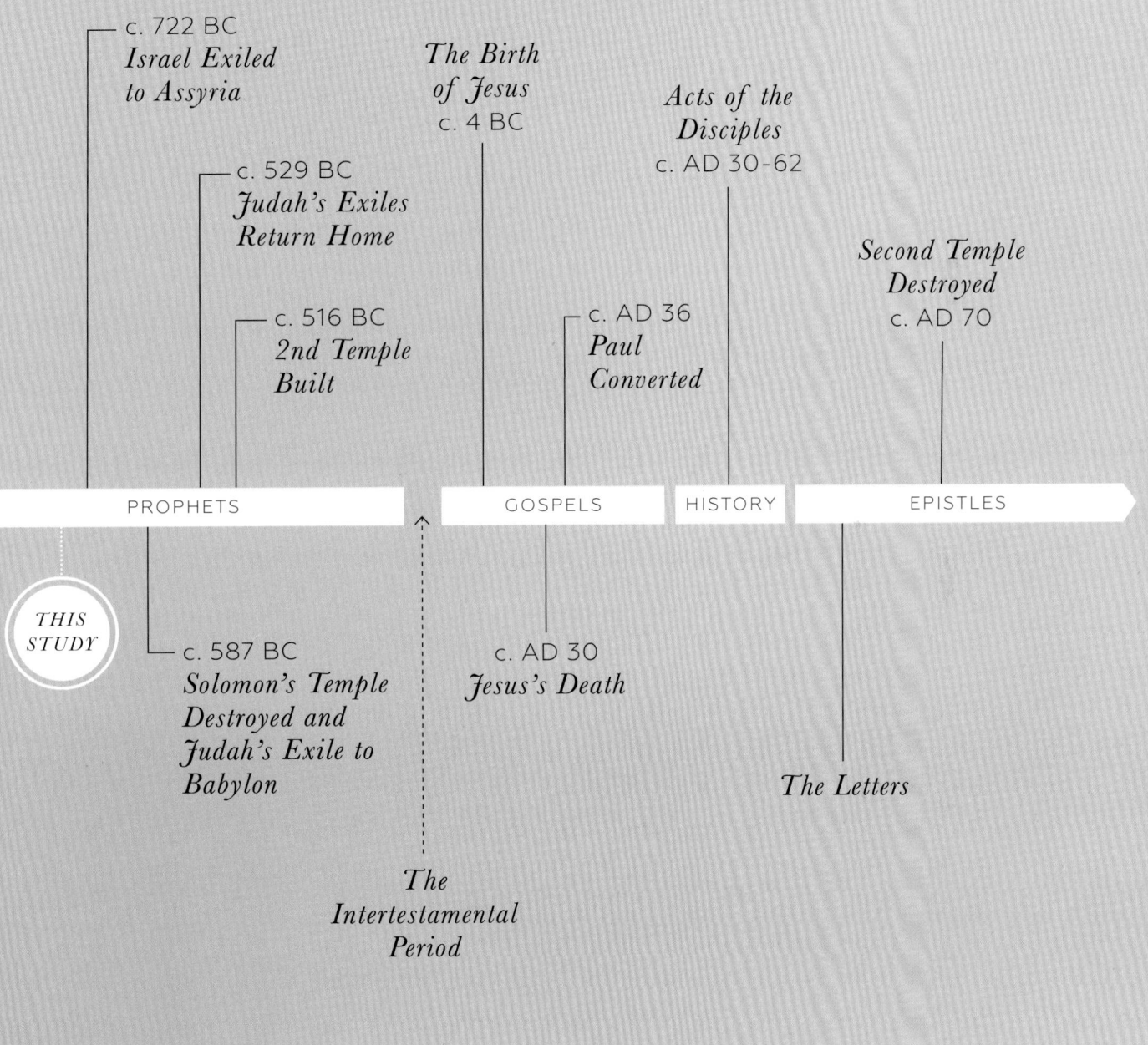

c. 722 BC
*Israel Exiled
to Assyria*

*The Birth
of Jesus*
c. 4 BC

*Acts of the
Disciples*
c. AD 30-62

c. 529 BC
*Judah's Exiles
Return Home*

*Second Temple
Destroyed*
c. AD 70

c. 516 BC
*2nd Temple
Built*

c. AD 36
*Paul
Converted*

| PROPHETS | GOSPELS | HISTORY | EPISTLES |

*THIS
STUDY*

c. 587 BC
*Solomon's Temple
Destroyed and
Judah's Exile to
Babylon*

c. AD 30
Jesus's Death

The Letters

*The
Intertestamental
Period*

Creation

In the beginning, God created the universe. He made the world and everything in it. He created humans in His own image to be His representatives on the earth.

Fall

The first humans, Adam and Eve, disobeyed God by eating from the fruit of the Tree of Knowledge of Good and Evil. Their disobedience impacted the whole world. The punishment for sin is death, and because of Adam's original sin, all humans are sinful and condemned to death.

Redemption

God sent His Son to become a human and redeem His people. Jesus Christ lived a sinless life but died on the cross to pay the penalty for sin. He resurrected from the dead and ascended into heaven. All who put their faith in Jesus are saved from death and freely receive the gift of eternal life.

Restoration

One day, Jesus Christ will return again and restore all that sin destroyed. He will usher in a new heaven and new earth where all who trust in Him will live eternally with glorified bodies in the presence of God.

in this study

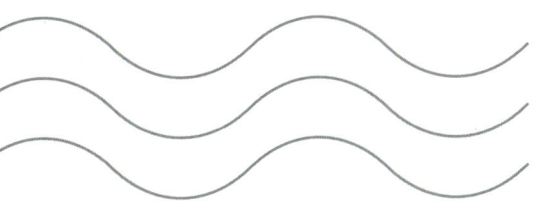

INTRODUCTION TO JONAH
Read Jonah 1–4

READ THE BOOK OF JONAH FROM START TO FINISH, AND ANSWER THE FOLLOWING QUESTIONS:

1. What key themes, words, or concepts did you notice in the book of Jonah?

_____

_____

_____

_____

_____

_____

_____

2. What did you observe about the character of God in the book of Jonah?

_____

_____

_____

_____

_____

_____

3. What questions do you have after reading through the entire book?

_____

_____

_____

_____

_____

_____

_____

_____

_____

_____

4. Write a prayer asking God to reveal more of Himself to you through this study.

_____

_____

_____

_____

_____

_____

_____

_____

_____

_____

_____

_____

_____

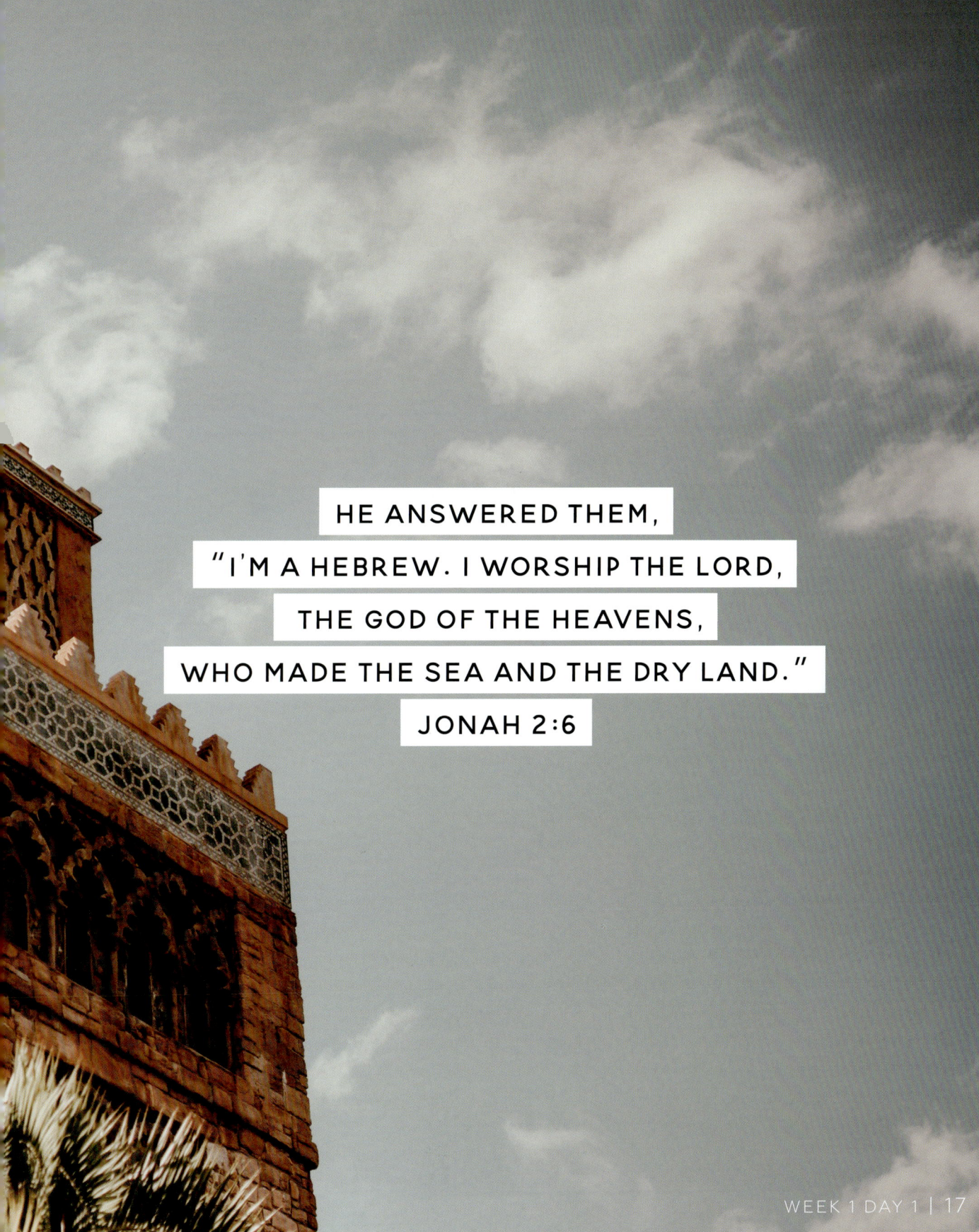

HE ANSWERED THEM,
"I'M A HEBREW. I WORSHIP THE LORD,
THE GOD OF THE HEAVENS,
WHO MADE THE SEA AND THE DRY LAND."
JONAH 2:6

THE STORY OF JONAH IS FIRST
AND FOREMOST A STORY OF
GOD'S MERCIFUL COMPASSION.

BACKGROUND TO JONAH

Read Jonah 1-4

The story of Jonah is one of the most widely recognized stories in all of Scripture. The tale of a man running from God is among the first Bible stories taught to toddlers in Sunday school, but this familiar book is about far more than a big fish. The story of Jonah is first and foremost a story of God's merciful compassion. It is a story that calls its readers to marvel at God's incredible kindness, examine their own hearts, and walk forward in obedience in light of His glorious character.

Jonah's authorship is unknown, but the consensus among scholars is that Jonah's own retelling of the events is the source for the book's content. It is one of the Minor Prophets, and while the possible dates of authorship range anywhere from the middle of the eighth century BC to the end of the third century BC, the book itself states that the events it recounts took place during the reign of Jeroboam II, who ruled from 782-753 BC.

It is helpful to review a brief Old Testament history up to this point to situate the book in its historical context. History began with the creation of the universe and humanity in Genesis. God's creation was good, but Adam's sin in the first chapter of Genesis resulted in the fall of man and the curse of death. From that time, sin spread like an infectious disease so that the fullness of man's heart and intentions were completely evil. Even as God pronounced the curse of sin in the garden, He promised a redeemer who would restore God's people and creation. Many years later, He made a covenant with a man named Abraham, promising that the Messiah would come through his offspring and be a blessing to the world. God's promise to make Abraham a great nation began to find its fulfillment as the Israelites, his descendants, multiplied to incredible numbers and became slaves in Egypt. God used a man named Moses to deliver them from slavery and into the wilderness. There, God made a covenant with them through the giving of the Law. Despite their frequent stumbling, God delivered them into the land He promised Abraham. The people were led by judges and kings, all proving themselves to be insufficient to rule God's people in righteousness, but God promised that a better king would come. God made a covenant with King David, promising that his offspring would rule righteously over God's people on an eternal throne. This promise would ultimately be fulfilled in Jesus Christ. The wickedness of the human kings who ruled over Israel led to the kingdom dividing into the Northern Kingdom, known as Israel, and the Southern Kingdom called Judah in 930 BC. Judah remained under the rule of Davidic kings. Eventually the wickedness and rebellion of both kingdoms would lead to their exile from the Promised Land in 722 BC and 586 BC.

The events of the book of Jonah take place during the reign of these kings whose sinful leadership eventually leads to exile. As a prophet to the Northern Kingdom (2 Kings 14:23-27), Jonah was God's instrument to call the Israelites to repent and return to the Lord. In the book of Jonah, God calls Jonah to bring His message, not to Israel but to a pagan nation. This command reveals not only God's compassion for Gentiles but also Jonah's own hardness of heart toward those who are not like him.

The book of Jonah is unique among the Minor Prophets. Instead of taking the traditional form of a prophetic book, in which the author recounts the word that God has spoken to him, Jonah fits within the genre of a historical narrative. Pieces of literature in this genre do not include every detail of the events that took place, but the author carefully chooses what information to include in order to convey his intended message. This historical account of Jonah is a masterfully written piece of literature, wrought with irony, word play, and an intentionally arranged literary structure. The storyline is simple enough for the ears of a child yet possesses a magnificent complexity that communicates profound truths through skillfully employed literary devices. Jonah is didactic in nature, meaning it is intended to teach moral lessons, and the timeless message in this book offers invaluable instruction to the contemporary reader. The book falls into the category of historical narrative, but it contains other genres as well, such as the poetry of chapter 2. It is important to be aware of this shift when interpreting the passage and consider the role of figurative language in the passage in contrast to the more literal retelling of the rest of the book.

In addition to God's compassion, the book of Jonah covers themes such as obedience to God, trusting in His character, and His sovereignty over all. It confronts sins like racism, nationalism, self-righteousness, and idolatry. Whatever our experience with the book of Jonah, we should come to it with minds that are ready to learn new things, hearts humbled before the Lord to hear what He might reveal about our hearts, and expectation to be in awe of the compassion of our good and holy God.

QUESTIONS

What was the extent of your understanding of the story of Jonah before beginning this study? What new insights do you have after reading it a second time?

_____

_____

_____

_____

_____

_____

_____

How does the background to the book of Jonah help you understand the narrative?

_____

_____

_____

_____

_____

_____

_____

The book of Jonah has important lessons to teach all of us. Write a prayer asking God to soften your heart to the sanctification He will do in you through His Word.

_____

_____

_____

_____

_____

_____

_____

JONAH RUNS FROM GOD BECAUSE HE DOES NOT TRUST IN HIS GOODNESS AND WISDOM.

RUNNING FROM GOD

Read Jonah 1:1-3, Psalm 139:1-12

The book of Jonah opens in typical fashion for a Minor Prophet by announcing the words of the Lord, which came to His prophet. While other prophetic books would proceed by recounting the message from God, this book takes a different turn. Rather than obey God's command to take His message to the Ninevites, Jonah runs, and the narrative that unfolds reveals much about the nature of God and the sinful heart of man.

The city of Nineveh was the capital of Assyria, one of the most powerful empires of its day, notorious for its unmatched cruelty, violence, and oppression (Nahum 3:1-4). Although the author does not yet reveal Jonah's reasons for refusing to bring God's instruction to the Ninevites, the historical context provides some clues. To go into a city known for wickedness and violence and pronounce God's impending judgment upon them for their evil deeds could put Jonah in harm's way. Moreover, bringing the words of the Lord to this pagan nation would be considered a terrible political move from the perspective of nearly all Israelites. Assyria was an enemy of Israel, and other prophets had warned that it would be at the hands of the Assyrians that the Israelites would be exiled (Hosea 11:5, Amos 4:2), a prediction that would become a reality not many years later in 722 BC. To warn the Ninevites of God's judgment could mean the preservation of a terrorist nation that would eventually demolish the Northern Kingdom, and yet, God tells Jonah to go on an unprecedented mission: to bring His message to a Gentile nation.

Instead of arising and going to Nineveh as God commanded, which was a relatively short trip, Jonah does the opposite. Jonah flees from his hometown of Gath-Hepher to the city of Joppa in order to board a boat to Tarshish, which was the furthest reaches of the known western world (see map on page 19). The repetition in these first few verses emphasizes Jonah's intentions—his heart is bent on disobedience. In verse 3 alone, the author repeats the word "Tarshish" three times and the phrase "away from the presence of the Lord" twice, making it abundantly clear that Jonah is not going to Nineveh, but he is doing everything he can to escape God's presence.

Why does Jonah flee? It is apparent that Jonah fears the personal and national implications of following God's commands, but at the heart of these fears likely lies something deeper—a lack of faith. Jonah runs from God because he does not trust in God's goodness and wisdom. Like Adam and Eve in the garden, Jonah believes that God does not have his best interest in mind. The tragic truth of rebelling against God's commands is that sin never leads to a more fulfilling life but to death. The word "down" is repeated several times in these opening verses, a word that was a euphemism for death. This theme of Jonah going further and further down is one that will continue throughout the narrative. In fleeing from God's presence, Jonah runs away from the very One who is the source and sustainer of life. Jonah may believe that his own fulfilled desires would result in a better life, but he fails to recognize the truth that God's concern for the wellbeing of His own is far greater than Jonah's. Thankfully for Jonah, God pursues His children, even when they turn their backs on Him. Jonah's story could easily end in death, but God chooses to show him mercy.

Because of his disobedience, Jonah fears the presence of God. In Psalm 139, David speaks about God's omnipresence, which he cannot escape. While Jonah sees God's omnipresence as something to flee, David rightly understands it as a reason to rejoice. Even when the reasons for the circumstances of this life are unclear, there is great comfort in the abiding presence of the good, sovereign, and merciful God. He is not malicious or cruel but kind and compassionate. No detail is outside of His control and fatherly compassion for His children, and He is always near.

Jonah's attempt to escape God's presence may seem foolish, but the reality is that every single one of us falls into the same pattern. The ways we run might not be so obvious, but we certainly run. We nurture hidden sin in our lives and attempt to hide from God's gaze by filling our days with church attendance or religious activity. We flee the call to love our neighbors and enemies by avoiding those who are difficult to love or demonizing them as an excuse to withhold compassion. We struggle with doubt, pain, or bitterness and avoid opening God's Word because we are afraid of what we might find there. If we are in Christ, God is not our enemy but our refuge. We are safe in His presence and safe in His will. We may not understand why God has allowed a particular set of circumstances in our lives, but we can rest in His goodness. We do not need to understand God's reasons in order to obey Him; we need only to trust that all His ways are good.

> ## THERE IS GREAT COMFORT IN THE ABIDING PRESENCE OF THE GOOD, SOVEREIGN, AND MERCIFUL GOD.

QUESTIONS

Jonah doubted God's wisdom in what He commanded him to do. In what circumstances are you tempted to doubt God's wisdom?

_____

_____

_____

_____

_____

How are you running from God? How can Psalm 139:1-12 be an encouragement to you rather than a reason to despair?

_____

_____

_____

_____

_____

Read Philippians 2:1-11. How does the example of Christ challenge Jonah's justification for disobedience?

_____

_____

_____

_____

_____

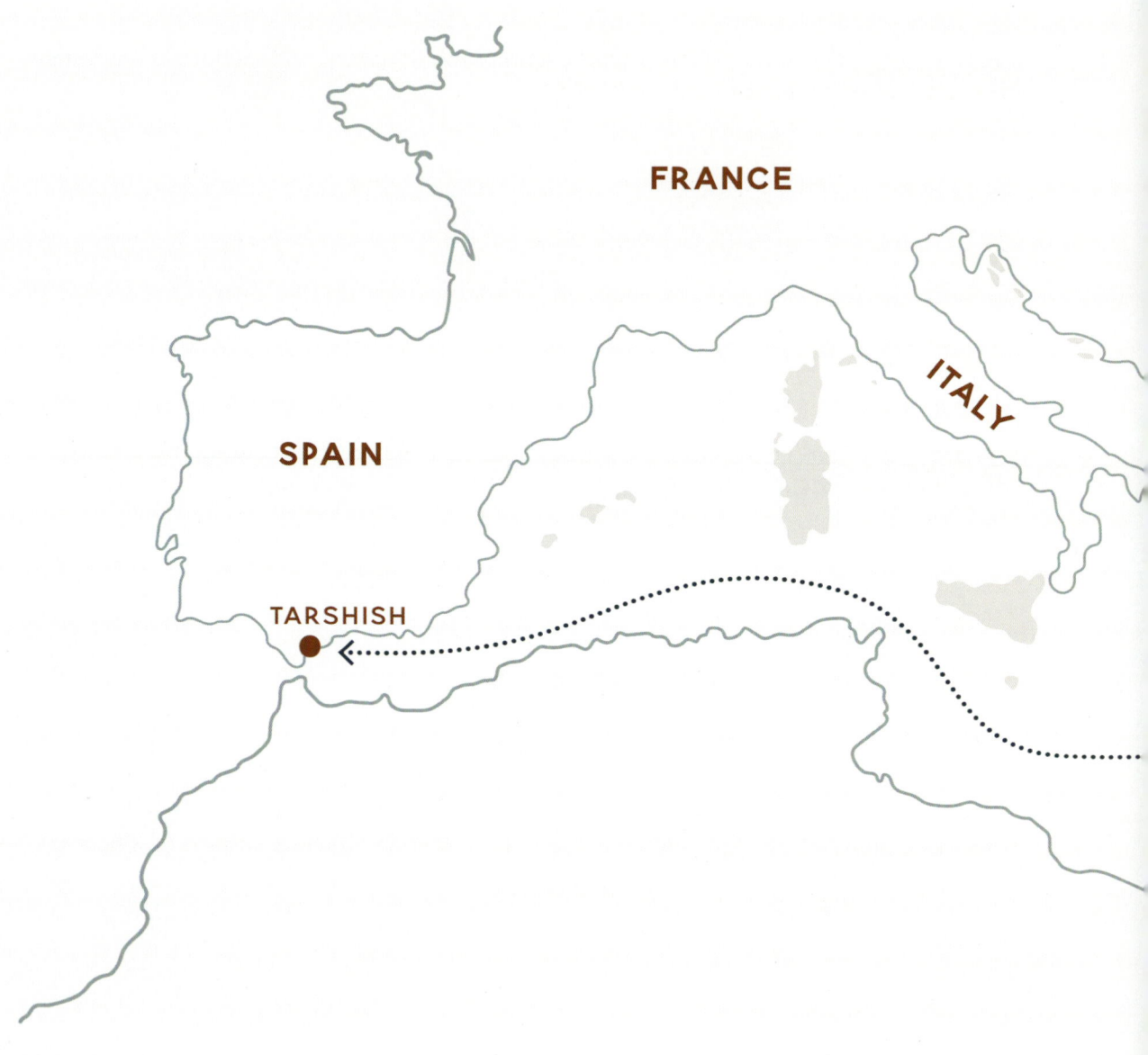

FRANCE

ITALY

SPAIN

TARSHISH

JONAH'S JOURNEY

TURKEY

ASSYRIA

THE MISSION ⋯⋯⋯→ ● NINEVEH

THE FLIGHT ←⋯⋯

ISRAEL

BABYLONIA

GATH-HEPHER

JOPPA ● ○ JERUSALEM

JUDAH

EGYPT

JONAH TRIES TO RUN AWAY FROM GOD,
BUT GOD IN HIS MERCY INTERVENES.

A STORMY INTERVENTION

Read Jonah 1:4-6

Jonah thought that he could escape the Lord's presence and commands, but God has other plans. Up to this point, Jonah's plan seems to be working. He boarded the boat to Tarshish and headed in the opposite direction of Nineveh, but it does not take long before the Lord intervenes.

With Jonah aboard the ship, God sends a great wind upon the sea that makes it abundantly clear that Jonah will not escape so easily. This is no small storm but a violent tempest with winds so great that the boat itself is in danger of breaking into pieces. Tossed by the crashing waves as the storm rages about them, the experienced sailors, who have no doubt weathered their fair share of storms, are rightly terrified, fearing for their very lives. Verse 5 reveals that the mariners on the ship are pagans, not worshiping the one true God of Israel but each calling out in desperation to his own god with no success. Their attempts to hurl their cargo into the sea to save themselves prove to be no match for the wind God has hurled upon the waters.

While the storm rages in a mighty display of God's power, Jonah hides away down inside the ship, seemingly indifferent to the peril of the sailors above. While the sailors futilely cry out to their gods to save them from imminent death, with no power to save themselves, Jonah is the only one whose God has the power to calm the stormy sea. Yet Jonah is asleep and inattentive to the wellbeing of his fellow man. In Jonah's sin, he is fleeing from God's presence and going down, down, down toward death, and now the captain finds Jonah in a sleep so—deep that the Hebrew word used here often indicates that someone has died. To turn away from God's presence could mean death not only for Jonah, but for those around him who are so desperately grappling for life.

In the tragically ironic scene that plays out next, it is the pagan sailors, not the prophet of God, called to represent Him and deliver His word. They serve as an example of fearing the Lord and responding to Him rightly. The captain of the ship appeals to Jonah for help with the very command that God gave him in verse two, "Arise!" Just as God's initial call, this plea is an appeal to arise and draw near to God instead of fleeing from His presence. It is a call to arise and show compassion to those whom God has created in His own image. Jonah is unconcerned with whether his shipmates live or die, but it is the pagan captain who urges him to have compassion and appeal to God on their behalf.

Jonah tries to run away from God, but God in His mercy intervenes. A tumultuous storm may seem less than merciful, but God uses it to save Jonah from a more devastating end—life apart from God. Jonah cannot see it from his limited vantage point, but God's call would ultimately be for Jonah's good. God could have left Jonah to deal with the consequences of his own decisions. He could have let him walk away from God's saving presence and down to a place where he would find only death, but God does not abandon His people. God pursues Jonah when he is running away, and He will continue to pursue him, not because He needs Jonah but because He loves him.

Like Jonah, we often doubt that God's will is for our good. The commands of God seem to be things that will stifle our joy instead of deepening it. We look around at the circumstances of our lives and question whether following God is worth all the pain. As we struggle from our place of limited understanding, we must remember the truth that God's will, no matter how confusing or painful it may be, is always for the good of His own. Still, we doubt that He is good and desires good for us, and if left to our own devices each one of us would turn away from Him. Praise God that He pursues us in our brokenness and sin. He is sovereign over the wind and the sea and all of creation, and He is sovereign over us. He will go to incredible lengths to save us from ourselves. God is a God of mercy, and He is merciful to us, even in our suffering.

> ❝
>
> God's will, no matter how confusing or painful it may be, is always for the good of His own.

QUESTIONS

Read back through Jonah 1:1-6. What repeated words did you notice in these first six verses? What do you think the author is trying to communicate in each case of repetition?

_____

_____

_____

_____

_____

_____

How does the author use irony to reveal Jonah's sin? How do you see your own sinful tendencies reflected in Jonah?

_____

_____

_____

_____

_____

_____

What difficult circumstances in your life might God be using to draw you back to Him? Are you using the opportunity to return to God, or are you finding a way to distract yourself and escape God's prompting?

_____

_____

_____

_____

_____

JONAH MAY CLAIM TO FEAR THE LORD, BUT FAITH IS LIVED OUT IN ACTIONS.

I FEAR THE LORD

Read Jonah 1:7-10

Jonah and the sailors have found themselves in the middle of a storm so tumultuous that the experienced mariners, who are likely well practiced in remaining calm and collected in bad weather, become frantic and panicked as they desperately search for a way to save themselves from certain death. The severity of the storm leads the sailors to the inevitable conclusion that this is no ordinary storm but the working of a greater power in response to some injustice. The sailors are correct in their recognition that sin merits judgment, and the storm is indeed God's response to Jonah's sin, but as the rest of the book reveals, God's judgment toward Jonah will not be without mercy. It is in fact through the storm that God will deliver him from the far greater storm raging in his soul.

In order to discover the culprit whose sin has resulted in the tempest, the sailors cast lots. This common practice in this time period functions much like drawing straws and relies on a divine force to determine the outcome. God is sovereign, even over the drawing of lots (Proverbs 16:33), and when the lot falls on Jonah, his guilt is exposed to his company. At this point in the text, questions may arise in the mind of the reader about the advisability of employing this practice today. While God uses this practice to convict Jonah in this instance, it should not be viewed as a model to imitate but as a description of a common practice in Jonah's day. Believers today have access to the complete canon of Scripture through which God speaks, as well as the indwelling of the Holy Spirit to teach, direct, and convict. There is no reason to rely on the rolling of dice because God has given to us His Word and His wisdom, which is far more superior.

As soon as the lot falls on Jonah, the sailors begin to question him. With the storm still raging around them, the sailors desperately try to discover the cause of this calamity so that they might find an antidote as they begin to ask Jonah identifying questions about who he is, where he comes from, and what his occupation is. In the answer that follows, Jonah not only gives the information they request but a critically important creedal statement about the God whom He serves.

Jonah identifies himself as a Hebrew who fears the Lord. He uses the proper name for God, *Yahweh*. The word order in the original Hebrew text places *Yahweh* as the first word of the clause, a tactic used to emphasize the word as one of primary importance. *Yahweh* means "I Am." He is the self-existing God without beginning or end. He is the one true God whose existence precedes the existence of all else. He is the God who is, and He is the only God who could bring about the force of nature surrounding the sailors. Jonah goes on to describe Him as the God who made the sea and the dry land. This is a literary device called a merism that implies that God is responsible not only for the creation of the two extremes of ground and water but of everything in between—He is the Creator of all things.

The reader can only imagine the terror that befalls the sailors with the realization that the very One who is sovereign over all of creation, the very God who made the sea that threatens them, is the One against whom Jonah is rebelling. The already present fear of the sailors multiplies as they come to terms with the reality of sin in the presence of the holy God. In keeping with the irony of this passage, while Jonah claims to fear the Lord, it is the sailors who exhibit genuine fear, while Jonah's actions indicate the opposite. The fear of the Lord produces wisdom in the life of believers (Proverbs 9:10), but Jonah follows earthly wisdom instead of displaying the wisdom of God. Fearing God is closely tied to keeping His commandments (Ecclesiastes 12:13), but it is the captain whose words recall God's command that Jonah has so foolishly rejected. The one who fears the Lord turns away from evil (Job 28:28), but Jonah turns away from the One who is wholly good. The fear of the Lord enables someone to turn away from the snares of death (Proverbs 14:27), but Jonah willingly goes down, down, down to his death, while it is the sailors who call him to concern himself with the lives of his companions. Jonah may claim to fear the Lord, but faith is lived out through actions.

We may claim to fear the Lord, but many times we behave as if we do not. Our daily choices and the way we respond to God's Word can often indicate that we fear many other things before God. Our failure to give generously reveals that we fear the future more than the God who provides. Our unwillingness to speak the truth in love to our brothers and sisters in Christ uncovers our fear of man. Our refusal to turn from our sinful patterns exposes a lack of fear of the Lord that leads us to believe that satisfaction can be found apart from Him. To fear the Lord—to regard him with reverence and awe for who He is—is to walk in obedience to Him. Yet frequently we fail, and so the Christian life must be a life marked by confession and repentance to the God who is willing and able to forgive us and transform us.

**TO FEAR THE LORD IS TO
WALK IN OBEDIENCE TO HIM.**

QUESTIONS

What does the storm reveal about God's character?

_____

_____

_____

_____

_____

_____

_____

What are some areas of your own life where your actions demonstrate that you fear something else more than you fear God?

_____

_____

_____

_____

_____

_____

_____

Read 1 John 1:9, and write a prayer confessing areas of disobedience in your own life and asking God to help you to grow in those areas.

_____

_____

_____

_____

_____

_____

I called to the LORD in my
distress, and he answered me.
I cried out for help from deep
inside Sheol; you heard my voice.
You threw me into the depths,
into the heart of the seas,
and the current overcame me.
All your breakers and your
billows swept over me.

JONAH 2:2-3

WEEK ONE REFLECTION

REVIEW JONAH 1:1-10

Paraphrase the passage from this week.

_____

_____

_____

_____

_____

_____

_____

_____

What did you observe from this week's text about God and His character?

_____

_____

_____

_____

_____

_____

_____

_____

_____

_____

What does this week's passage reveal about the condition of mankind and yourself?

_____

_____

_____

_____

_____

_____

_____

_____

_____

_____

How does this passage point to the gospel?

_____

_____

_____

_____

_____

_____

How should you respond to this passage? What specific action steps can you take this week to apply this passage?

_____

_____

_____

_____

_____

Write a prayer in response to your study of God's Word. Adore God for who He is, confess sins that He revealed in your own life, ask Him to empower you to walk in obedience, and pray for anyone who comes to mind as you study.

CHRIST MAKES A WAY FOR MERCY.

JUDGMENT AND MERCY

Read Jonah 1:11-13

Jonah's guilt has been discovered, and now the sailors must decide how to proceed in their desperate situation. Tension rises as the already terrifying storm intensifies and the need for a solution becomes increasingly urgent. The mariners, likely in a state of overwhelming terror, turn to Jonah with their seemingly impossible question, "How do we make this stop?"

Given Jonah's dismissive and rebellious attitude up to this point, his response may seem a bit surprising. The sailors must throw him into the raging sea. Just as God has hurled the storm upon the sea, so Jonah must be hurled into the sea in order for it to calm. For the first time in this already eventful narrative, Jonah begins not only to take responsibility for his own actions but to show some concern for the welfare of those who are not like him. Perhaps the storm sent from God is already beginning to produce transformation for the better in Jonah's heart.

Jonah has come to terms with the fact that He is in the wrong and that his sin is the reason that this calamity has come upon him and his company. Jonah rightly recognizes that his sin merits God's wrath, and so he believes that the only way for the sailors to be spared is for Jonah, the sinner, to be destroyed. However, as the unfolding narrative will show, God in His mercy will not only remove His wrath from the sailors but also spare Jonah's life. This grace is possible for Jonah and all who will call upon the name of the Lord, only because of the work of Jesus Christ on the cross.

Jesus Christ is the second person of the Trinity, the fully divine Son of God who became a man in order to save sinners like Jonah. All humans are sinful and are therefore condemned to death and subject to the wrath of God (Romans 3:23, Romans 6:23). Apart from Christ, God's wrath would mean that Jonah would have been consumed by the raging sea that day. Likewise, every person would face the same fate of death without hope of new life, but Christ died in the place of sinners so that they could have the life He earned in His sinlessness. Christ makes a way for mercy, so God's wrath falls not on sinners but on Christ in the place of sinners. This substitutionary atonement—the blood of Christ paying the price of death in the place of those who put their faith in Him—applies to those like Jonah who believed in the promise of His future coming, as well as those who put their faith in Him after His life, death, and resurrection. Instead of putting Jonah to death, God would work to put to death Jonah's sin, sanctifying him, changing his heart, and making him more and more holy through the trials of his life.

Jonah told the sailors what they must do to save themselves, but the sailors are hesitant to follow his advice. As has been the case throughout chapter 1, the pagan mariners ironically continue to function as a picture of the kind of mercy and compassion Jonah should have exhibited all along. Up until this moment, Jonah showed no regard for the well-being of others,

whether it be the Ninevites or the sailors, yet it is they who work to prevent harm from coming upon Jonah, possibly at the expense of their own safety. This behavior is to be expected from someone like Jonah, who has experienced the unmerited grace of God. Jonah's failure to extend that same grace is underscored in contrast to the pagan sailors who cannot be expected to do so. Try as they might, the sailors cannot row their way back to safety. While the storm certainly appears to be devastating, God has plans to use it for Jonah's good, and nothing can stop His sovereign plans.

Jonah is beginning to show signs of transformation, but He still has a long way to go. Sanctification can be slow, but God is faithful to use every circumstance in our lives, including the painful ones and the storms, to purify us from sin and make us more like Him.

―――――― 66 ――――――

God has plans to use it for Jonah's good, and nothing can stop His sovereign plans.

QUESTIONS

Read Romans 6:23 and 1 Peter 3:18. What would our fate be apart from Christ? How does Christ offer hope for Jonah and for us?

_____

_____

_____

_____

_____

_____

How should experiencing the grace of God impact the way you treat others? What are some ways you fail to extend the same grace that was given to you in Christ to others?

_____

_____

_____

_____

_____

_____

Jonah begins to show signs of transformation, but the process is slow. As you look back over your own life, how have you seen God work sanctification in you through the difficult circumstances of your life?

_____

_____

_____

_____

_____

_____

HE IS OUR HOPE. HE IS OUR COMFORT.
HE IS OUR JOY AND OUR PEACE
IN THE CALM AND IN THE STORM.

KINDNESS IN THE STORM

Read Jonah 1:14-16

The sailors have tried everything in their own strength to escape the terrors of the storm, but they are powerless against the God who created the very sea that rages against them. With all other options exhausted, they turn and call out to the Lord. For the first time in the text, the pagan sailors use God's proper name, *Yahweh*. The description of the sailors calling out to the one true God stands in stark contrast to their actions in verse 5 when each of them called out to his own god. They petition the Lord to save them and not hold the death of Jonah against them.

As the sailors plead with God to spare their lives, they appeal to Him by saying that God has done as He pleased. As Thomas Bolin points out, the language of God doing as He pleases occurs three other times in the Old Testament, and in all three cases, the passages emphasize God's sovereignty as well as the powerlessness of idols and other gods. In light of these texts, the sailors' language indicates a new understanding about the God of Israel. He is the only One who is sovereign. He is the only One who is powerful. He is the only One who can bring the storms and make them cease in a moment. Their gods cannot help them, but their help comes from the Lord alone. As soon as they pick Jonah up and throw him into the sea, their newfound faith is confirmed; the storm calms just as quickly as it arose.

As Jonah's fall into the sea results in the safety of the sailors, Jonah serves as a picture of a greater One to come whose death would be the source of rescue. He points forward to Jesus, reflecting some part of His work or character, albeit imperfectly, giving glimpses of the One who would be the perfect rescuer. In Jonah's case, the sailors were subject to the wrath of God's judgment, but through the sacrifice of one man, Jonah, many sailors were spared from imminent death. While in Jonah's case the judgment was a result of his own sin, the sinless Christ would suffer, not on His own account, but He would take on the sins of humanity and bear God's judgment as a substitute to save many. While the sacrifice of Jonah saved the mariners from the peril of the storm, only the once-for-all sacrifice of Christ is effective to save souls from death and into eternal life.

The sailors have seen the mighty works of the Lord. They have experienced how fierce His judgment is for sin and tasted His extravagant mercy. They have witnessed His unopposable power and have been recipients of His tender grace. They have seen the terrible might and gentle kindness of the Lord, and they have not gone unchanged. While their fear has increased in proportion to the intensifying storm, their fear in the calm is greater now than it has been all along. Now the object of their fear is not the storm that threatened to take their lives but the God who has the power to enact judgment and extend mercy. Their fear has found its proper place as they revere the Lord God, evidenced by sacrifice and taking vows, actions indicative of those whose hearts have turned to fear the Lord.

The book of Jonah is one that highlights God's mercy, compassion, and kindness toward humanity, and this passage is no exception. God shows Himself to be a God who brings people into His family. Jonah believes that salvation should be only for himself and his people. When God sends Jonah to bring His word to the Ninevites, he runs away, but unbeknownst to Jonah, God in His sovereignty sends him to these pagan sailors so they might fear the Lord

and experience His mercy. Surely, God's kindness is displayed in the calming of the storm, but the nature of His compassion runs deeper. The mariners come to fear the Lord, not only because He rescues them from the storm but because He sends the storm in the first place. God graciously interrupts the rhythm of their lives with hardship so that they might clearly see their need for Him.

We all see our fair share of storms in this life. We experience suffering that seems unbearable and pain that can make us cry out to God in desperation saying, "God, You said that You cared for me. You said that Your love is steadfast. You said you would be kind to me. So why are you letting all these things happen to me?" But sometimes God's kindness is the storm. You may not understand why God has sent a storm into your life, but you can be sure that God is transforming you into His image in the midst of every one. No matter how confused we may be about the circumstances of our lives, our response to each storm should be to turn to God. He is our hope. He is our comfort. He is our joy and our peace in the calm and in the storm. The mariners did not turn to Him at first, and we are often quick to turn elsewhere as well, but God pursues us even if it means pain along the way, for the joy He has for us is far better.

YOU MAY NOT UNDERSTAND WHY GOD HAS SENT A STORM IN YOUR LIFE, BUT YOU CAN BE SURE THAT GOD IS TRANSFORMING YOU INTO HIS IMAGE IN THE MIDST OF EVERY ONE.

QUESTIONS

How did seeing the character of God produce change in the sailors?

_____

_____

_____

_____

_____

_____

_____

When you face struggles in this life, where do you tend to turn for help?

_____

_____

_____

_____

_____

_____

_____

God showed His kindness to the sailors by sending the storm. How does this truth encourage you in your own life?

_____

_____

_____

_____

_____

_____

_____

JESUS IS THE BETTER JONAH.

THE TWO STORMS

Read Jonah 1:4-16, Matthew 8:23-27, Mark 4:35-41

Reread the account of the storm in Jonah, and read the two accounts of Jesus calming the storm. Compare and contrast the events that take place in these passages, and mark the similarities and differences in the chart below.

JONAH IN THE STORM (JONAH 1:4-16)	JESUS CALMS THE STORM (MATT. 8:23-27, MARK 4:35-41)

The account of the storm God sends upon Jonah reveals God's sovereignty and mercy and also exposes Jonah's own sinfulness. This man who is supposed to be God's representative has fallen terribly short of His calling. Jonah leaves us looking for a better prophet who will not run from God's will but will walk willingly in it—One whose sin will not bring wrath but whose righteousness will bring salvation.

Two passages in the New Testament bear a striking resemblance to the events of Jonah 1. In Matthew 8 and Mark 4, the Gospel writers recount the story of another boat, another storm, and another sleeping prophet. The remarkable similarities between both events that transpire and the language the authors use certainly would have caused the original readers of the Gospels to recognize meaningful connections between the two incidents that occurred around 800 years apart.

All three passages describe a previously calm sea suddenly struck by a great and windy storm. Just as was the case with Jonah and the mariners, the boat that houses Jesus and His disciples is beaten by violent waves so strong that the boat can hardly hold together. The mariners and the disciples become anxious and afraid and seek the help of the respective prophets, Jonah and Jesus, both of whom are sleeping inside the boat. The tone of rebuke in the captain's voice as he addresses Jonah is echoed in Mark's account of the storm as the disciples question whether or not Jesus cares if they live or die. It is at this point in the narratives that the parallels diverge, emphasizing the very important difference between Jonah and Jesus and revealing important truths about the character of Jesus.

In Jonah's case, his interrogation led to continued rebuke from the sailors for his sin and, ultimately, his self-proclaimed sentencing to a watery death. In contrast, at this point in the accounts of Jesus's storm, Jesus rises and rebukes the storm. He commands the winds and the waves to be still, and instantly the sea is calm. The disciples are awestruck at this miraculous sight, asking the question, "Who is this man?"

This rhetorical question is one we are invited to answer for ourselves. What kind of man speaks and even the winds and the waves obey him? Who is this man who utters a word, and the stormy sea ceases from its raging? Is the One who is sovereign over the sea and the dry land not the One who made them both? Is it not the Lord God who brings the winds from His storehouses (Psalm 135:7)? Who is this man? He is God Himself. He who calms the storm with the words, "Silence! Be still," is the same One who commanded the ocean to quiet down when Jonah was hurled into the sea. The responses of great fear and awe from the sailors and the disciples are both evidence of the same realization: they have witnessed the work of the almighty God. How then will we respond to Him?

On the one hand, the remarkable parallels between these two stories attribute the sovereignty of God displayed in Jonah 1 to Jesus Christ, demonstrating His divinity as the Lord who is to be feared. On the other hand, these similarities also reveal Jesus as the better Jonah. Jonah's sin is the reason the sailors are in danger of dying, but Jesus came to save sinners from death, just like His disciples on the boat. They are both confronted with essentially the same question, "Don't you care if we die?" It is a question that reveals Jonah's lack of compassion and powerlessness to save the sailors but exhibits the kindness and power of Jesus as He intervenes on the disciples' behalf. Jesus did not need to be thrown into the sea for it to cease from its raging so that the disciples' lives could be spared, but it is His substitutionary death that would bring about eternal salvation. Jonah is a prophet whose call is to go between God and man by bringing them His word, but instead He runs away. Jesus is the better prophet and intermediary who not only brings God's word, but also is the Word of God incarnate, willingly submitting even unto death so that the saving word of God will come to fruition.

Jonah's voyage on the sea leaves our hearts longing for a better intermediary and a better prophet, and those longings find their fulfillment in Christ. When Jesus calms the storm, He turns to His disciples and asks them why they are afraid. Is their faith still so small? Do they not know who goes with them? They are led by the fully divine Son of God who has authority over all creation. What then should they fear? It is when their fear takes its proper place, directed to God alone, that all other fears fall away. As we read the story of Jonah, may our minds and hearts look to Christ.

> "
>
> Jesus is the better prophet
> and intermediary who not only brings
> God's word, but also is the Word.

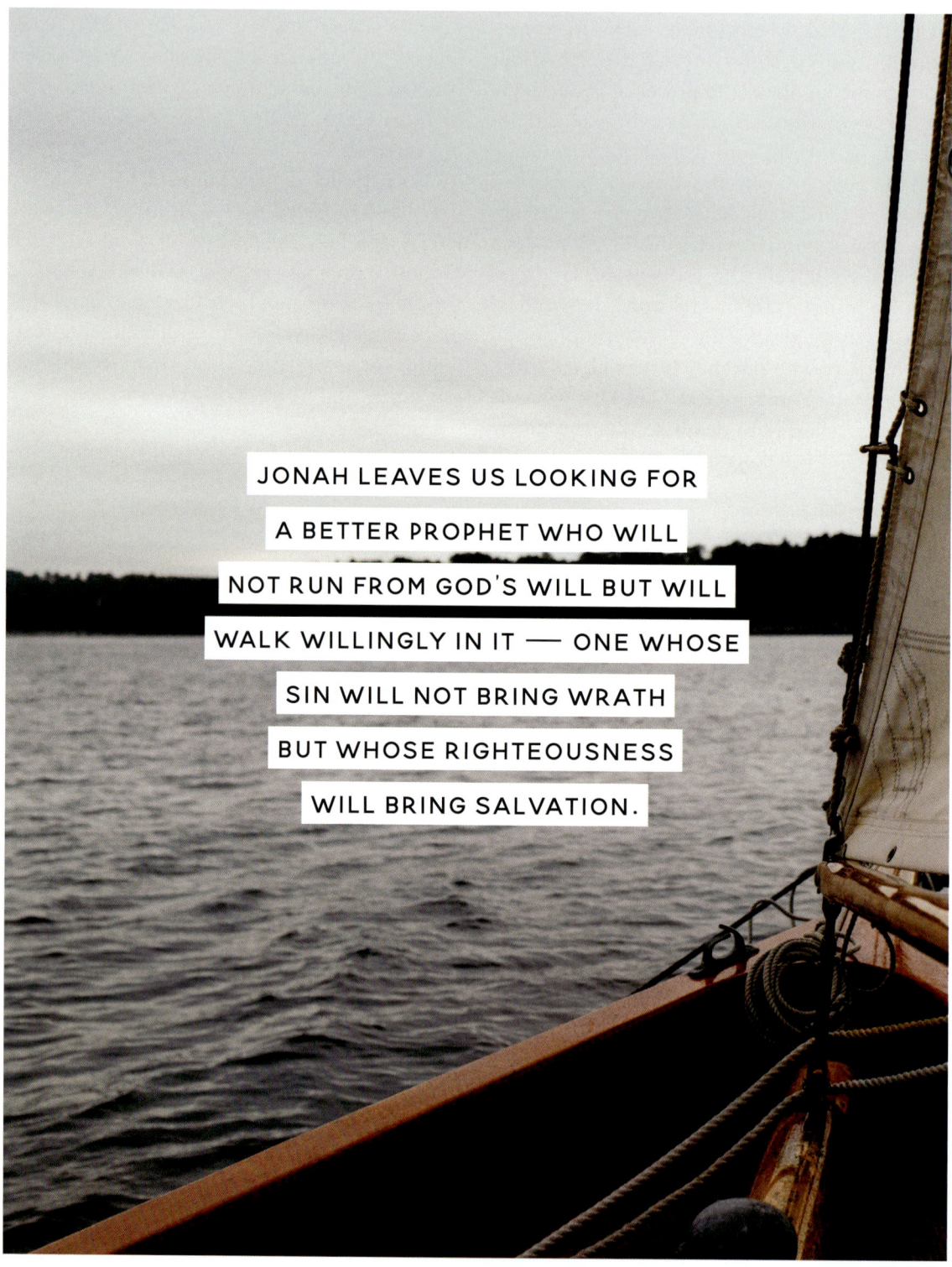

JONAH LEAVES US LOOKING FOR
A BETTER PROPHET WHO WILL
NOT RUN FROM GOD'S WILL BUT WILL
WALK WILLINGLY IN IT — ONE WHOSE
SIN WILL NOT BRING WRATH
BUT WHOSE RIGHTEOUSNESS
WILL BRING SALVATION.

QUESTIONS

What do the similarities and differences between the accounts of Jonah's storm and Jesus's storm reveal about Jesus Christ?

_____

_____

_____

_____

_____

_____

_____

How do Jonah's shortcomings increase your longing for Christ?

_____

_____

_____

_____

_____

_____

_____

What are you currently afraid of? How would fear of the Lord inform the way you respond to those fears?

_____

_____

_____

_____

_____

_____

_____

THERE IS NOTHING OUTSIDE OF THE CONTROL OF THE ALL-POWERFUL GOD.

SOVEREIGN GOD

Read Jonah 1:17, Psalm 135:1-7

The narrative, focused on the unlikely characters of the pagan mariners and their encounter with the almighty God, now shifts its focus back to the book's main character, Jonah. Jonah has been thrown into the raging sea, a death sentence by any human standard, but God is not finished with Jonah.

The text says that God appointed a great fish to swallow Jonah. This use of the word "appointed" is the first of four that occurs in this book and indicates God's sovereignty over creation. To say God is sovereign means He is in complete and total control over everything. He is not a God who simply creates and then leaves the universe to its own devices, but He is intricately involved with even the tiniest details of His creation, orchestrating it all for His good purposes.

Throughout the course of the narrative up to this point, the author has been emphasizing God's sovereignty over creation. It was God who threw the wind upon the sea and brought about the storm in verse 4. The sailors' attempts to call out to their own gods in verse 5 were futile, because only the Lord is sovereign. Jonah emphasized God's role in the storm by describing Him as the Creator of all things in verse 9. The sailors' inability to row back to the shore underlined the power of God over the ocean. It was God who caused the storm to stop instantly in verse 15. The message throughout this chapter is clear—there is nothing outside of the control of the all-powerful God. Nothing and no one can resist His will. Try as he might, Jonah cannot run away from God's plan, and God will use even the sea and the dry land to accomplish His purposes. He does all that He pleases, and His good will is accomplished.

Now the narrative highlights another miraculous display of God's sovereignty as He appoints a great fish to swallow Jonah. The Hebrew word for fish is a much more general classification than the modern English term, so the species could be a large fish, a whale, or some other type of sea creature. Not only is this event a demonstration of God's power, but also of His mercy. Jonah's stay in the belly of the fish will not lead to his death, but this unlikely vehicle is a source of God's rescue. Jonah's three day and three night stay in his watery prison without food or fresh water may not seem like grace at the time, but God has plans to work even in this uncomfortable near-death experience. God certainly could lift Jonah out of the waters and place him on dry land unharmed, but there is far more at stake than Jonah's physical comfort and safety. God intends to transform his very heart.

Oftentimes, God's grace shows up in surprising ways, and we may fail to recognize what He has ordained as His kindness. We may find ourselves in a dark season of our own that from our vantage point seems as if it could only lead to harm. We could be blissfully unaware that we are sinking down toward our death, and God's unglamorous rescue feels like an unwelcome and painful interruption. Perhaps we are on day two in the belly of our own fish without any idea of how it could possibly end well. Our vision is obstructed inside the apparatus of God's rescue, but He is outside of it all, working all things together in His sovereign hand for His glory and our good. No matter what pain and darkness we experience as God's children, none of it is outside of His fatherly care for us. Even the pain is His instrument of grace.

> "
> He is intricately involved with even the tiniest details of His creation, orchestrating it all for His good purposes.

QUESTIONS

How does Psalm 135 describe God's involvement with creation (verses 5-7), and how should we respond to it (verses 1-4)?

_____

_____

_____

_____

_____

_____

_____

How does God appointing the fish show the correlation between His sovereignty and goodness that is highlighted in Psalm 135?

_____

_____

_____

_____

_____

_____

What pain or difficulty are you experiencing or have you experienced in the past that is or was difficult to see as a source of God's grace? How can looking back on your own life and on God's character in Scripture encourage you in dark seasons?

_____

_____

_____

_____

_____

_____

_____

HE CALLED UPON THE LORD IN DISTRESS, AND GOD ANSWERED HIM.

THE GOD WHO HEARS & ANSWERS

Read Jonah 2:1-2

This chapter opens with Jonah praying to God from inside the fish, which turns out to be an instrument of God's mercy instead of His wrath. Although later chapters will show that Jonah's heart is still in need of significant sanctification, chapter 2 is evidence of his continual transformation as a result of God's pursuit of Jonah.

Chapter 2 marks a shift, not only in Jonah's perspective but also in the literary style of the text. While the book is presented as a historical narrative, chapter 2 interrupts the normal flow of the storytelling to document Jonah's prayer, which falls under the genre of poetry. Jonah's prayer bears a striking resemblance to the biblical psalms. Taking the genre of a text into account should significantly impact the interpretation of the passage. Poetry, by nature, is marked by figurative language and vivid imagery, so while the narrative portion of the book of Jonah presents events as they occurred, the poetry in chapter 2 requires a much less literal interpretation.

The entirety of chapter 2 is written in a chiastic structure, meaning that the ideas expressed in the first half of the prayer are paralleled in reverse order in the second half (see the chiastic outline below). This literary structure serves to illustrate the radical nature of God's rescue of Jonah that completely reverses Jonah's apparent fate. Jonah's situation declines to the point of near death until he reaches his lowest point at the center of the chiasm in Jonah 2:5-6. The remainder of the prayer mirrors the first half as God intervenes to rescue Jonah from his lowly state.

> A. *The Lord sends a fish to swallow Jonah and Jonah begins to pray (1:17-2:1)*
>> B. *Jonah calls out to God in distress from Sheol (2:2)*
>>> C. *Jonah descends down into the sea and closer to death (2:3-4)*
>>>> X. *Jonah is at his lowest point (2:5-6a)*
>>> C. *God pulls Jonah up from the pit (2:6b)*
>> B. *Jonah calls out to God in rejoicing from His temple (2:7-9)*
> A. *The Lord commands the fish to vomit Jonah out (2:10)*

As Jonah sits in the belly of the great fish, he begins to pray to the Lord. Up until this point, he has been running away from God, but now he draws near. The pagan sailors ironically urged him to pray, something that Jonah should have been doing already. But now, having escaped certain death by God's mercy alone, he prays of his own accord. Although the extent of Jonah's heart transformation is uncertain, it is clear that something is changing. He has seen the wrath and mercy of the Lord and, as a result, he is not the same.

The content of Jonah's prayer is remembrance and thanksgiving. The past tense verbs indicate that Jonah is not praying for deliverance from the fish but is thanking God for deliverance from the depths of the ocean by means of the fish. Jonah recalls that when he was at his lowest point, he called upon the Lord in distress, and God answered him. God could have justly left Jonah for dead, but even though Jonah directly rebelled against God, even though his sin brought calamity upon those around him, and even though Jonah's own actions led to his horrific journey toward death, God answered him.

An understanding of the abundant literary devices in the prayer illuminates much of the meaning of the passage. The parallelism of the two couplets in Jonah 2:2 emphasizes the grace of God's action on Jonah's behalf—Jonah called, and the Lord answered. Jonah cried, and God heard his desperate pleas. Jonah says he cried out from the depths of Sheol, known as the place of departed souls—the residence of the dead—from which no one could escape. Jonah does not imply that he experienced a literal death, but he uses hyperbole to communicate that he was so close to death that there seemed to be no escaping it. The word that is sometimes translated as "depth" can also be translated into its literal meaning, "belly." The author uses personification, attributing human characteristics to nonhuman things, to describe this place of death as hungry for Jonah. The play on words between "depth" and "belly" points to Jonah's unexpected rescue from one belly, the belly of Sheol, to another, the belly of the fish.

Jonah's words reveal a truth about God's character that provides great comfort. God hears, and God answers. Just as God heard Jonah's prayer from the depths of the ocean, we are never too far from the Lord to call upon Him. God rescues when we call out to Him, even when we have rejected Him and rebelled against Him, even when the trouble from which we need to be rescued is because of our own sin, and even when we have neglected to seek Him in the past. God's mercies are not limited by our inadequacies. Do not tarry to cry out to Him. Do not say, "I have wronged Him too much. I cannot ask Him to rescue me now." You are never too far gone to receive His mercy. God rescued Jonah from death, and He died for us when we were dead in our sins. The Lord desires to show compassion, and His extravagant grace cost Him the life of His only Son, so do not reject it. Call upon the Lord. He hears, and He answers.

WE ARE NEVER TOO FAR FROM THE LORD
TO CALL UPON HIM.

QUESTIONS

How does understanding the literary style of today's passage deepen your understanding of its meaning? How should this approach impact the way you study all of Scripture?

_____

_____

_____

_____

_____

_____

What does today's passage reveal about God? How do these aspects of His character give you hope in your own life?

_____

_____

_____

_____

_____

_____

_____

What prevents you from calling out to God in your own desperation? How can Jonah's story encourage you to turn to God?

_____

_____

_____

_____

_____

_____

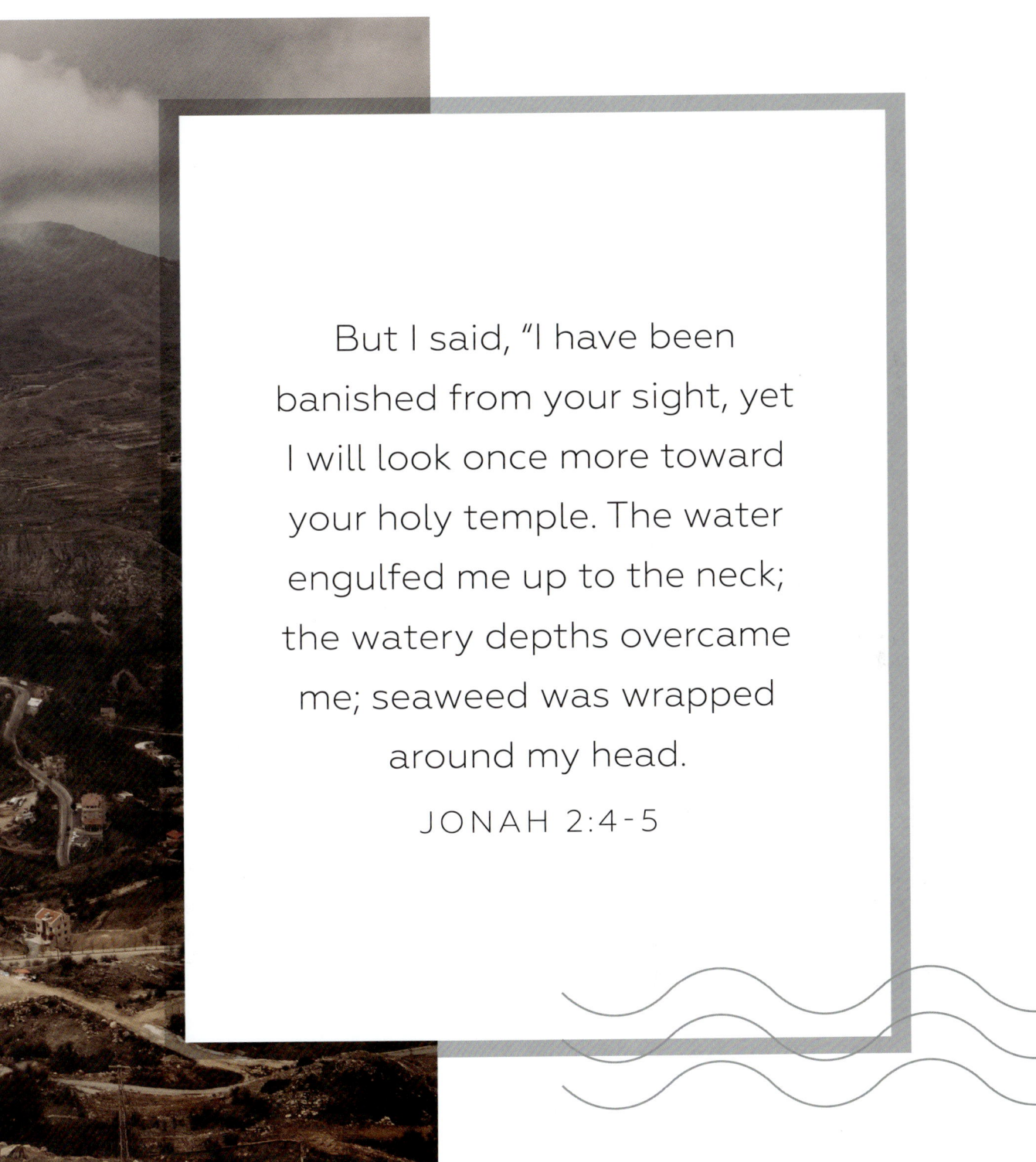

But I said, "I have been banished from your sight, yet I will look once more toward your holy temple. The water engulfed me up to the neck; the watery depths overcame me; seaweed was wrapped around my head.

JONAH 2:4-5

WEEK TWO REFLECTION

REVIEW JONAH 1:11 - 2:2

Paraphrase the passage from this week.

_____

_____

_____

_____

_____

_____

_____

_____

_____

What did you observe from this week's text about God and His character?

_____

_____

_____

_____

_____

_____

_____

_____

_____

What does this week's passage reveal about the condition of mankind and yourself?

_____

_____

_____

_____

_____

_____

_____

_____

_____

How does this passage point to the gospel?

_____

_____

_____

_____

_____

_____

How should you respond to this passage? What specific action steps can you take this week to apply this passage?

_____

_____

_____

_____

_____

_____

Write a prayer in response to your study of God's Word. Adore God for who He is, confess sins that He revealed in your own life, ask Him to empower you to walk in obedience, and pray for anyone who comes to mind as you study.

JONAH'S HOPE IS NOT
ESCAPING GOD'S PRESENCE
BUT RETURNING TO IT.

WEEK 3 DAY 1

A HUMBLING DESCENT

Read Jonah 2:3-4

Jonah calls out to the Lord in prayer from the belly of the fish in Jonah chapter 2, and in the next two verses, he begins to describe his descent into the ocean. The entire prayer, and this section in particular, is wrought with vivid aquatic imagery that communicates Jonah's sense of despair and helplessness during his journey down into the ocean as he is plunged toward death.

In these verses, Jonah highlights God's power and sovereignty as he attributes the affliction that has beset him to the hand of God. Although it is the sailors who physically threw Jonah into the sea, he recognizes that God is the ultimate source of his expulsion. Likewise, Jonah describes the waves that came down upon him as God's billows and breakers. God made the sea, He controls the sea, and now He has commissioned the sea against Jonah. Although Jonah knew the fact of God's sovereignty intellectually as evidenced by his description of God as the Creator of the sea and the dry land in Jonah 1:9, Jonah's own experience of God's power against him has caused him to be acquainted with God's sovereignty in an intimate way. For Jonah, God's sovereignty is no longer simply a doctrine to proclaim but a humbling and transformative reality. This God whom Jonah claims to fear is a God of holy wrath with all of creation at His disposal. This God, against whom Jonah so audaciously rebelled, has the power to take life, but He also has the power to give it. He is a God of wrath and mercy, and now Jonah is faced with the terrifying reality that he has pridefully turned from the will of the One whose will cannot be thwarted. It was in this humbled state that Jonah cried out to God for mercy.

These two verses are replete with water imagery that poignantly illustrates the terror and hopelessness that Jonah experienced when he was hurled into the sea. We are invited to imagine the crushing pressure of the water as Jonah was plunged into the depths of the sea, his powerless struggle as the ocean current overtook him, and his breathless descent as wave after wave forced him down. This kind of aquatic imagery appears throughout Hebrew poetry to describe someone who is in a state of incredible distress. For Jonah, this language

WEEK 3 DAY 1 | 67

describes not only his physical reality but the turmoil of his own heart. This is a man who has been overcome by inescapable anguish, a man who finds himself at the brink of death with seemingly no chance of escape.

The thought of a painful physical death, although terrible, was not the primary reason for Jonah's distress. With the breath forced out of his lungs and the light in his eyes dimming, Jonah lamented that he was driven away from God's sight. The terror of death is not Jonah's lungs filling with water and his heart stopping but separation from the presence of the holy God. Jonah, who had been running away from God's presence, believing escape from God's will to be in his own best interest, came to dread the prospect of being hidden from God's sight. His brush with death called his heart back to the reality that God's will is always good, and His presence brings fullness of joy (Psalm 16:11).

Even as Jonah despaired of the hope of God's presence, he called his soul to remember the character of God. God's presence seemed to be slipping away from him, but Jonah quickly made a declaration of faith and hope with the word "yet." It may seem as if all hope is lost, yet God is faithful. The pain may feel like too much to bear, yet God is merciful. Jonah believed and proclaimed that even though it seemed as if God had abandoned him, yet he

would again look toward God's holy temple. The temple is especially significant in this passage because the temple represented the presence of God. The temple was God's dwelling place through which God dwelt among His people. Jonah's hope, then, is not in his escape from God's presence but His return to it. The wrath of God has come against Jonah, and the merciful result is that Jonah's perspective has shifted to see rightly the attitude he should have toward God's presence.

We may find ourselves in a situation where it seems as if we are out of God's sight. The suffering of this life can make it feel like God has abandoned us in our pain, but because of Jesus, we can say with confidence that God is with us. Christ became a man, the very embodiment of God with us, and bore the wrath of God against sin so that we could dwell with Him. Even when painful experiences pummel us like crashing waves dragging us along the ocean floor and disorienting us so that we cannot catch our breath, we can declare this truth to our hearts: "I will again rejoice in the presence of the Lord." God does not abandon us, but He pursues us, and it is often through our pain that He draws us near to Himself. God has promised His presence to us, and He has guaranteed it by the death and resurrection of His Son. His presence is the greatest gift of salvation, and it is our hope in every situation.

IT MAY SEEM AS IF ALL HOPE IS LOST, YET GOD IS FAITHFUL.

QUESTIONS

What does today's passage reveal about God's character?

_____

_____

_____

_____

_____

_____

_____

How has Jonah's attitude toward God changed from chapter 1 to chapter 2?
What factors do you think contributed to this change?

_____

_____

_____

_____

_____

_____

_____

Are you experiencing anything currently, or have you in the past, that made it seem as if God abandoned you? What truths about God can you preach to yourself in these situations?

_____

_____

_____

_____

_____

_____

_____

THE GOD WHO RESCUED JONAH
IS THE SAME GOD WHO RESCUES US.

THE GOD WHO COMES DOWN

Read Jonah 2:5-6

Today's passage marks a glorious turning point in Jonah's psalm to the Lord. Verse 5 and the first half of verse 6 mark the center of the chiastic structure. Jonah has been describing his descent into the ocean, and now these verses illustrate Jonah's lowest point at death's door, but God in His mercy would not leave him there.

Jonah uses stunning imagery to show the depths of his distress with the description of his physical position on the ocean floor mirroring his psychological state. The language of the waters closing in over Jonah contributes to the sense of Jonah being pulled further down without any power to keep his head above the water until he is totally surrounded by the ocean's depths. The roots of the mountains describe the bottom of the ocean floor with the seaweed wrapped around his head serving as a picture of Jonah's inability to escape death as the branches tie him down like chains. It is not necessary to consider these descriptions as literal. Jonah may not actually have journeyed to the deepest part of the sea, but this imagery reflects the reality that Jonah had descended to the lowest point of his life and was helpless to pull himself out of his distress.

Throughout the narrative, the author has emphasized that Jonah has been going down, an expression intended to suggest that Jonah has been barreling toward death. He went down to Joppa to escape the Lord's presence, down into the ship, and now in verse 6, this motif continues as Jonah describes the point where he could go down no more. He found himself at the very point of death. He went down to the land whose bars closed upon him forever. This language refers once again to Sheol, the land of the dead whose entrance is guarded by barred gates and from which no one can depart once they have entered. The center of the chiastic structure of this prayer has brought Jonah as far down as he can go. He is as good as dead, but at his lowest point, things are about to change.

Once again, Jonah's despair is interrupted graciously as his descent down to death turns to a raising up toward life. Jonah was completely helpless to save himself, yet the Lord his God rescued him. Jonah rejoices with thanksgiving to God as he uses His proper name, *Yahweh*, a name employed six times in this passage alone. *Yahweh*, who breathed life into dust to form Adam, is the same God who gave life to Jonah when he was at the brink of death. This *Yahweh* who rescued Noah from the destruction of the flood also pulled Jonah from the flood that engulfed him. The very same *Yahweh* who delivered the Israelites through the Red Sea out of the bondage of slavery freed Jonah from the chains of death that held him in the ocean. Jonah knew about the works of this *Yahweh*, but now he has personally experienced the unchanging character of the merciful God.

The God who rescued Jonah is the same God who rescues us. Jonah could never muster the strength to swim to the surface of the waters, ascending above his own sin, but the Lord pulled him up. For all those who are in Christ, we share Jonah's story. God descended to us in the midst of our brokenness and depravity, humbling Himself, leaving His glory, and becoming a man so that He might lift us out of the pit. Jonah 2:6 paints a picture of Jonah as good as dead, yet God raised him up. In the same way, Paul says in Ephesians 2 that we were dead in our sins, but God in His great mercy and love made us alive in Jesus Christ. Oh, that we would look into God's Word and see our own reflection in Jonah, hopeless in the face of death but pursued and rescued by our merciful Savior!

Even at our darkest, we are not too far from God's reach. We may feel as if we are too far gone, but the Lord's arm is not too short or too weak to save us (Isaiah 59:1). We may find ourselves feeling stuck in our own brokenness and sin, like Jonah pinned to the ocean floor, but even though we are helpless to save ourselves, God is able to rescue, and He rescues all who call upon Him (Romans 10:13). We cannot reach up to Him, but God in His grace comes down to us.

―――――――――――― 66 ――――――――――――

Jonah was completely helpless to save himself, yet the Lord his God rescued him.

QUESTIONS

What do you think it would have been like to be Jonah in those moments?
Have you ever felt this way?

_____

_____

_____

_____

_____

_____

Read Ephesians 2:1-10. How does the character of God displayed in Jonah 2:5-6 point forward to the hope we have in Jesus Christ?

_____

_____

_____

_____

_____

What area of your life do you believe to be out of God's reach? Write a prayer asking God to bring redemption.

_____

_____

_____

_____

_____

_____

MAY IT BE THAT IN OUR OWN STORMY SEAS, WE REMEMBER THE LORD AND HIS MERCY,

REMEMBER THE LORD

Read Jonah 2:7-10

Jonah's very life was slipping away from him. There was no escape from certain death, and all hope seemed lost. But, in that moment, Jonah remembered the Lord. The word "remember" in this passage does not mean that God suddenly popped into Jonah's mind, like remembering we left the oven on as we rush out the door, but this type of remembrance is intentionally calling something to mind. As Jonah felt the life leaving his body, he remembered *Yahweh*. He called to mind the one true God who is sovereign over the seas and dry land and has power over life and death. He reminded himself of the One who shows steadfast love and mercy to those who call upon Him, and even from his place of utter brokenness, he prayed.

Though Jonah prayed from the depths of the seas, his prayer went into God's holy temple. The temple represents the presence of God. Even when Jonah found himself as far down as he could go, God's presence did not depart from him. Just as the psalmist proclaims in Psalm 139, even in the depths of sheol, in the uttermost parts of the sea, God's presence remains and holds fast to His beloved.

Jonah thinks back to sailors as he declares that to cherish idols is to turn away from God's steadfast love. Jonah rightly recalls the futility of their calling out to their own gods to save them, knowing that it is only *Yahweh* who can save. Ironically, even the sailors turned to call out to the one true God before Jonah did, taking hold of the steadfast love of the Lord who showed them mercy, Gentiles though they were. Jonah's prayer once again echoes back to the actions of the sailors when he speaks of making sacrifice and vows to the Lord. God used the storm to bring about transformation in the sailors, and now that same kind of transformation is taking place in Jonah. Jonah recognizes that calling out to idols is futile because only the Lord saves, but the rest of the narrative will show that Jonah still holds onto his own idols, not of wood or stone but of his own flesh and blood. Jonah has idolized his own comfort and well-being from the beginning of the story, attempting to make himself God as he ran from *Yahweh*. The rest of the story will reveal that his prideful self-idolatry still lingers in his heart.

Jonah's declaration that salvation belongs to the Lord is a faith statement that stands in contrast to his actions at the beginning of the narrative. Jonah thought he could save himself from God's will by running away from His presence, believing God's will to be not for Jonah's good but something that would bring him harm. Now Jonah has been humbled by the Lord, and he comes to understand that God is the only One who can bring about true salvation. Jonah may have thought he was saving himself, but he was actually on the path of destruction that leads to death. God in His mercy intervened, though painfully, to bring Jonah back to Himself. God's pursuit produces repentance, and repentance is a life-saving gift, even when it comes at great cost. When Jonah's prayer ends, God commands the fish to vomit Jonah onto the dry land, a clear demonstration of the truth that Jonah just uttered: salvation belongs to the Lord. God's sovereignty over creation is once again evident, and Jonah is rescued from death through a humbling and merciful ordeal.

This section of Jonah began with God calling the fish to swallow Jonah, and it ends with God commanding it to vomit him onto dry land. The chiastic structure of the prayer emphasizes the reality of how God extended grace to Jonah, as well as how His mercy often manifests toward us. God brings low in order to raise up again. He wounds that He might heal. Our suffering may be bitter, but God's grace is sweet. These words from Charles Spurgeon are especially poignant in light of Jonah's rescue, "I have learned to kiss the wave that throws me against the Rock of Ages." May it be that in our own stormy seas, we remember the Lord and His mercy, that we call out to Him, and that we look back from the other side and rejoice because of God's mercy in the storm.

"

He reminded himself of the One who shows steadfast love and mercy to those who call upon Him, and even from his place of utter brokenness, he prayed.

QUESTIONS

All throughout Scripture, God calls us to remember who He is and what He has done, like Jonah did in his prayer. What characteristics of God can you call to mind as you remember Him in your current circumstances?

_____

_____

_____

_____

_____

_____

Read Psalm 139:7-12. What does this passage reveal about God's character, and how is that character displayed in Jonah 2?

_____

_____

_____

_____

_____

_____

Can you think of a time in your own life or in the life of someone else when God used suffering as a source of mercy? How can that experience and the story of Jonah encourage you in your own struggle?

_____

_____

_____

_____

_____

_____

GOD HAS BEEN AND WILL ALWAYS BE FAITHFUL.

RESTING ON THE WORD OF GOD

Read Jonah 2:2-9, Psalm 18:1-19, Psalm 42

Reread Jonah's prayer, and read the two psalms of David.
Compare Jonah's prayer to the psalms, and mark the similarities in the chart below.

JONAH 2:2-9	PSALM 18:1-19	PSALM 42

Jonah's prayer in chapter 2 bears a striking resemblance to psalms such as Psalm 18 and Psalm 42, among others. The Psalms were written before the events in the book of Jonah took place, and as a Hebrew prophet, Jonah certainly would have been very familiar with them. In his time of distress, Jonah draws from the Word of God as grounding for his own prayer.

Much of the content of Jonah's prayer closely mirrors that of Psalm 18. David describes his situation as he feared for his life with imagery of the ropes or cords of death and Sheol wrapping around him (Psalm 18:4-5). Jonah likely draws from this psalm when he describes himself as being in the depths of Sheol, as good as dead, with the seaweed wrapped around his head at the bottom of the ocean floor. This psalm also employs aquatic imagery by referring to the torrents of death in verse 4 and God pulling him up from out of the waters in verse 16, much like Jonah's description of God pulling him up from the pit and the bottom of the sea in Jonah 2:6. Both speakers describe their prayers as reaching God in His temple in order to indicate that God is always present and always hears. Both David's psalm and Jonah's prayer emphasize that salvation comes from the ever-present God who answers those who call out to Him for help.

Jonah's prayer also seems to be heavily influenced by David's prayer in Psalm 42. In this psalm, David describes his deep longing for the Lord's presence. David cries out as he feels that God has forgotten him (Psalm 42:9), much like Jonah's declaration that God has banished him from His sight (Jonah 2:4). In the midst of their despair, both call their hearts to remember the Lord and place their hope in Him. David's refrain, "Put your hope in God," is echoed by Jonah's remembrance of the Lord as his

life was fading away and his declaration that even though it seems God is not near, he will look again on God's temple. Perhaps the most striking similarity between Psalm 42 and Jonah chapter 2 is Jonah's exact quotation of Psalm 42:7, which says, "all your breakers and your billows have swept over me." Not only did these words literally ring true in Jonah's physical situation, but they also express his own emotional state, which corresponds with that of David.

When Jonah was tempted to despair, he rested in the faithfulness of God, evidenced in His Word as a steady anchor for his weary soul (Hebrews 6:19), and we can learn from this example. The Bible is the story of God working to bring about His plan of redemption. As we study His Word and become more familiar with that story, we will see the faithfulness of the unchanging God on every page. And that truth is the anchor that holds us in confident hope as we are thrown about in our own stormy seas. Consistently coming to the Word of God is a discipline. The benefits far surpass obtaining factual knowledge about the Bible, but as we read, study, memorize, and meditate on God's Word, those truths take root in our hearts, becoming the foundation of our hope that the Holy Spirit calls to mind in our time of need (John 14:26).

In his moment of repentance, Jonah also models something that many other men and women of God throughout Scripture and church history have modeled: praying Scripture. As we pray God's Word, we learn to appeal to Him based on His revealed character. In doing so, our hearts are directed to pray for the things that God values, and we find comfort in knowing that others have struggled as we have, but God has been and will always be faithful. The Psalms in particular are an excellent example of how we can pray in the midst of distress. We pour out our hearts to the Lord, and then we remember who He is. The more we study God's Word, the more we will naturally pray His Word. The Word of God is a place where we can run to find refuge, comfort, and assurance in the character of God.

QUESTIONS

What characteristics of God did you see in today's readings?

_____

_____

_____

_____

_____

_____

_____

_____

Based on your own circumstances, write a prayer to God that incorporates some of the language, characteristics of God, and/or structure you noticed in today's readings.

_____

_____

_____

_____

_____

_____

_____

_____

_____

GOD IN HIS MERCY GIVES
JONAH A SECOND CHANCE.

THE RECOMMISSIONED PROPHET

Read Jonah 3:1-4

After Jonah's psalm-like prayer in chapter 2, the story returns to its primary genre of historical narrative. As chapter 3 begins, it is as if the author returns to the beginning of the story and starts telling it all over again. In fact, the Hebrew text includes an indication to leave a blank space between the end of chapter 2 and the beginning of chapter 3. God commissioned Jonah to bring His word to the Ninevites in chapter 1, and now chapter 3 begins with Jonah's recommissioning.

Chapter 3 begins very similarly to the way chapter 1 began but with some important variations. After Jonah's humbling near-death experience and rescue by means of the fish, the word of God comes to him a second time. God could have sent someone else to fulfill the mission to Nineveh when Jonah so pridefully rebelled against His good commands. He could have given up on Jonah and left him to deal with the consequences of his sinful ways. He could have left Jonah to die in the raging sea, but God in His mercy gives Jonah a second chance. God does not need Jonah, but He intends not only to show mercy to the Ninevites but to Jonah as He transforms him. God does not give up on Jonah but is patient with him for the sake of his sanctification.

In verse 2, God repeats the command He gave to Jonah in Jonah 1:2 to call out against the city of Nineveh. Despite Jonah's sin, God's plans have remained the same. They cannot be thwarted. No imperfection or sinfulness of man can stand in the way of the holy purposes of the almighty God. The repetition of the command shows God's determination to bring His word to the Ninevites, a people who were not only outside of the Israelite community, but were wicked enemies. God's determination to bring near those who are far from him, even those outside of ethnic Israel, is evident in the conversion of the sailors, His command to Jonah to go to the Ninevites, and ultimately, in the death of His Son, Jesus Christ. The Lord would bring near those who are far off and adopt as His children people from every tribe, tongue, and nation.

Significantly, the second half of God's repeated command to Jonah is different than when He first called Jonah. This time God says, "Get up! Go to the great city of Nineveh and preach the message that I tell you" (Jonah 3:2). In God's fatherly discipline toward Jonah, He emphasizes to Jonah the importance of obedience to His command, whatever it may be. Jonah's obedience should not be conditional on the details of what God calls him to do, but Jonah's response to God's unchanging character should always be obedience, even if he does not understand God's reasons.

The opening verses of chapter 3 continue to parallel those of chapter 1 as verse 3 gives Jonah's response to God's call. Chapter 1 emphasized Jonah's rebellion against God's command. He got up and went the opposite direction to flee from the Lord's presence. Now in chapter 3 the narrator emphasizes Jonah's opposite response. This time, Jonah obeys. He gets up, as the Lord commanded him, and goes to Nineveh according to the Lord's command. Jonah's newfound obedience stands in stark contrast to his defiant rebellion at the beginning of the story. Although time will show that Jonah still has a long way to go in his own sanc-

tification, his response to God's call indicates a continued transformation in him. Jonah goes into Nineveh and begins to proclaim the message that Nineveh will be "overthrown" in forty days. The word overthrown in many translations can carry the meaning of being destroyed or of being transformed. It is possible that Jonah's words to the Ninevites, which he hoped would be indicative of their destruction, actually foreshadow the repentance of Nineveh.

In recommissioning Jonah, God has shown Himself to be a God who is patient and merciful. God did not give up on Jonah, and He does not give up on any of His children. Even when we fail, God can still use us. We do not have to live in the shadow of our past guilt because God redeems us and graciously uses us as His chosen instruments. God promises that He will complete the good work he began in us and that everyone whom He chooses He also works to make holy and blameless (Philippians 1:6, Romans 8:29-30). God's work through us is not based on our own goodness but on His. If you are in Christ, you can be certain that God is not finished with you yet.

No imperfection or sinfulness of man can stand in the way of the holy purposes of the almighty God.

QUESTIONS

What do the parallels between Jonah 1:1-3 and 3:1-3 reveal about the work God is doing in Jonah's heart?

_____

_____

_____

_____

_____

_____

In what area of your life are you hesitant to obey, and how can resting in God's character help you to obey?

_____

_____

_____

_____

_____

_____

Can you think of anyone else, either in Scripture, church history, or someone you may know whom God used despite their sin? How do these stories encourage you as you look back at your own mistakes?

_____

_____

_____

_____

_____

_____

I sank to the foundations of the mountains, the earth's gates shut behind me forever! Then you raised my life from the Pit, Lord my God! As my life was fading away, I remembered the Lord, and my prayer came to you, to your holy temple.

JONAH 2:6-7

WEEK THREE REFLECTION

REVIEW JONAH 2:3 - 3:4

Paraphrase the passage from this week.

_____

_____

_____

_____

_____

_____

_____

_____

What did you observe from this week's text about God and His character?

_____

_____

_____

_____

_____

_____

_____

_____

What does this week's passage reveal about the condition of mankind and yourself?

_____

_____

_____

_____

_____

_____

_____

_____

How does this passage point to the gospel?

_____

_____

_____

_____

_____

_____

How should you respond to this passage? What specific action steps can you take this week to apply this passage?

_____

_____

_____

_____

_____

_____

Write a prayer in response to your study of God's Word. Adore God for who He is, confess sins that He revealed in your own life, ask Him to empower you to walk in obedience, and pray for anyone who comes to mind as you study.

GOD LONGS TO SHOW MERCY IN RESPONSE TO REPENTANCE.

REPENTANT SINNERS, RELENTING GOD

Read Jonah 3:5-10

Jonah has experienced the merciful hand of God through his rescue from a watery death, been recommissioned to bring the word of the Lord to the evil Ninevites, and has finally responded in obedience. Now the Ninevites believe the Lord, and they repent.

The Ninevites' swift and dramatic response is shocking. This nation, notorious for its violence, cruelty, and wickedness, now shows itself to be a model of repentance in response to God's word. In the original Hebrew language, the first word of verse 5 is the word translated "believed," and the word order emphasizes the immediacy with which the Ninevites responded to God's warning. Much like the pagan sailors who respond rightly to the Lord while Jonah turns from Him in disobedience, wicked Nineveh ironically exemplifies the way that not only Jonah, but Israel as a whole, should respond to their own sin but has failed to do so. The king's hope that God may turn and relent directly echoes the words of the prophet Joel toward Israel in Joel 2:14. Moreover, 2 Kings 17:13-14 uses the language of Jonah 3:8 when the king of Nineveh calls the people to turn from their evil ways, but unlike the Ninevites, the people of Israel did not believe and did not listen to the word of the Lord. Jonah's own delayed obedience stands in stark contrast to the swift turning of the Ninevites as well. This contrast between God's chosen people and a nation known for their brazen sin serves as a convicting message to Jonah's Hebrew audience, as well as to contemporary readers who are so often slow to confess and repent from our own evil ways.

When the king of Nineveh hears word of the message Jonah delivered, he immediately repents and calls the entire nation to do the same. All of Nineveh, from the greatest to the least, even the king himself, humble themselves before the Lord. Nobody is above repentance. The content of the king's command and the people's response reveals an exemplary pattern of repentance. First, the Ninevites hear the word of the Lord, and they believe it. In order for genuine repentance to take place, people must believe God's Word, and in order for them to believe the Word, they must first hear it (Romans 10:17). Once the Ninevites are confronted with their sin, they mourn over it. They clothe themselves in sackcloth and sit in ashes, typical signs of grieving and mourning over personal sin, but they do not stay in their grief. Next, they call out to God, the One who has the power to enact judgment and show mercy, that He might show them compassion. Finally, they not only confess their sin, but they turn away from it. The word "repent" means "to turn," and true repentance is marked by obedience that comes from a changed heart. This model of hearing God's Word, believing God's Word, mourning sin, calling out to God, and walking in obedience is one all are called to imitate.

The role of the king in the repentance of the Ninevites is quite remarkable, and his own actions point forward to an even better king, Jesus Christ. The king of Nineveh stepped down from His throne and called his people to repentance, but the King of kings stepped down from a greater throne in heaven to call His people to repent and return to the Lord. The humility of the Ninevite king was merited as he saw his own sin and the sin of those around him in light of God's infinite holiness, but Jesus humbled Himself even though He was the infinitely holy Son of God, in order

that we might be saved from our sins. The king of Nineveh bore sackcloth and ashes as he called out to God on behalf of the Ninevites, but Jesus bore our sin and humbled Himself all the way to the point of death. When Jesus died on the cross, He absorbed the wrath of God that we rightly deserve in our sin. It is His death that enables the repentance of the Ninevites, the repentance of Jonah, and our own repentance. It is His sacrifice that makes a way for mercy. Jesus Christ is the better King.

When the Ninevites repent, God relents. God is not a God who delights in the death of the wicked but who longs to show mercy in response to repentance (Ezekiel 18:23). The Lord is compassionate. The God who showed kindness to Nineveh is the same God who has been working throughout all of history to show kindness to us. The first command of Jesus's public ministry in Matthew 4:17 was to repent, and it is a call to return to the Lord who will lavish us with grace and welcome us as His own. We are called to repentance, not just at the moment of our salvation but every day as we put our sin to death and turn to walk in obedience, knowing that when we confess our sins, the One who paid the highest price for our redemption will be faithful and just to forgive us and make us clean (1 John 1:9).

――――――― **"** ―――――――

Christ's sacrifice makes a way for mercy.

QUESTIONS

Read the verses below, and note what they reveal about sackcloth and ashes in relation to repentance:

Genesis 37:33-34 _____

_____

Esther 4:1-4 _____

_____

Nehemiah 9:1-3 _____

_____

Daniel 9:3 _____

_____

Read Psalm 51:17. Do you find that you mourn over your own sin? What does your attitude toward sin reveal about what you believe to be true of God and of yourself?

_____

_____

_____

What does God's response to the repentance of the Ninevites reveal about His character?

_____

_____

_____

How does today's passage point to Jesus?

_____

_____

_____

NO ONE IS DESERVING OF GOD'S MERCY, BUT GOD OFFERS IT ANYWAY.

MISPLACED ANGER

Read Jonah 4:1-4, Joel 2:12-14

At the end of chapter 3, all of Nineveh repented of their evil ways, and God showed them mercy instead of the judgment He threatened. Now in chapter 4 the narrative returns to Jonah, who is displeased with God's compassion for the Ninevites. The language that describes Jonah's anger indicates that he is furious and burning with anger. He views God's withholding of judgment as a great injustice and would rather die than live in a world where the Ninevites receive God's mercy. Although Jonah seems to have undergone some measure of transformation resulting in his delayed obedience, it is clear that his heart is still bent against God's will. Jonah's brush with death humbled him before the God of creation, but God still has more to teach him.

The opening words, "He prayed to the Lord," remind us of the first time he called out to God in chapter 2, but the content of these two prayers is dramatically different. In Jonah's first prayer, he expressed gratitude to the Lord for showing him mercy, but in this prayer, he burns with anger that the Lord would show that same compassion to the Ninevites. The prayer brings us back to the very beginning of the narrative, revealing Jonah's motive for resisting God's will—he knew God would show the Ninevites compassion. Jonah's own hypocrisy is revealed in the fact that he worshiped the God who saved his life and soul from death in chapter 2 and now begs God to take that same life from him because of the mercy He has shown the Ninevites.

Jonah's declaration of God's character as a "gracious and compassionate God, slow to anger, abounding in faithful love, and one who relents from sending disaster," is a direct quote from Exodus 34:6-7. Jonah knew that God would prove true to His character, and Jonah's suspicion was correct. The Ninevites turned from their sin and called out to the Lord with fasting, weeping, and mourning, and the Ninevite king hoped that God would turn and relent. God had proven His character to the Israelites, yet Jonah fails to see that measure of mercy as a reason to rejoice in that same mercy extended to others.

Jonah does not want the Ninevites to experience the mercy and compassion of God, and we may find that we share Jonah's sentiment. Have you ever had a sense of satisfaction when someone got what they deserved or felt frustrated and annoyed when they did not? Have you ever been hurt by someone and found yourself hoping that life would be difficult for them so they can feel the repercussions of their own wrongdoing? Have you ever secretly wished that someone would not find healing and forgiveness? Over and over again, Scripture calls us to forgive as we have been forgiven (Ephesians 4:32, Colossians 3:13), but like Jonah, we often want to withhold that mercy from others.

If we lack compassion for others, it may be that we do not understand the measure of compassion that God has shown to us. If we do not desire forgiveness for others, perhaps we have not realized our own wretchedness and the incredible grace that God has lavished upon us when we have so horribly offended Him. Jonah seems to see himself as somehow deserving of God's grace while the Ninevites are unworthy. Perhaps he compares his own sin to the wickedness of the Ninevites and thinks, "Surely I am not bad, and surely their sin is too great to receive God's mercy." But has not the book of Jonah been highlighting the depth of Jonah's sin by emphasizing all along that these people—the pagan sailors, the Ninevites—who may seem so much worse than Jonah are the very ones who become examples of what Jonah ought to be doing? Jonah may have the outward appearance of righteousness, but his heart is desperately wicked, and so are ours. If we see ourselves as deserving of grace and others as unworthy to receive it, then we have missed the beauty of the gospel. No one is deserving of God's mercy, but God offers it anyway. When we are honest about the depth of our own sin, we can rejoice in the extravagance of God's love and see God's character, not as something to despise but to adore.

Jonah ran from God because He did not want Him to be who He said He was. Jonah viewed God's character, not as something to delight in but as evil and unjust. Jonah could not understand how God could be good in showing mercy to a people who were so wicked, and his frustrations would be partially founded if not for the cross. When God declares His own merciful steadfast love in Exodus 34:6-7, He says that He will forgive sin and "will not leave the guilty unpunished." While these two statements may seem contradictory, they find their fulfillment in Christ. God does not leave sin unpunished, but for those who repent and believe in Him, He sets His wrath not on us but on Jesus Christ. At the cross, God's justice and mercy meet.

God questions Jonah's anger. As we read these words in verse 9, we should ask ourselves the same question. When we question God's plan, do we have a right to be angry? We may not see the whole picture, but God does. We may not understand how God's goodness is at play in the different circumstances of our lives, but we can believe that He is who He says He is, and who He is, is holy.

QUESTIONS

Is there anything that God says about Himself and His character that you don not like?

_____

_____

_____

_____

_____

_____

_____

Read 1 Samuel 16:7. How has the book of Jonah shown the severity of his inward sin despite his outward appearance?

_____

_____

_____

_____

_____

_____

_____

Write a prayer confessing some of the things for which God has forgiven you and thanking Him for His mercy.

_____

_____

_____

_____

_____

_____

_____

TRUE LOVE FOR GOD RESULTS IN LOVE FOR OTHERS.

WE LOVE BECAUSE HE LOVED

Read Jonah 4:5, Leviticus 23:33-43

The Lord has mercifully relented from destroying the city of Nineveh, but rather than rejoice in God's compassion, Jonah stews in bitterness. Jonah leaves the city, but does not immediately return home. Although the Lord has spared Nineveh, Jonah is still waiting and hoping for their destruction. He goes east of Nineveh, opposite the way he entered, to a hilly region where he can safely look down on the city and see what he hopes will be their gruesome end. He builds himself a tent and waits to see what God might do to the city.

Jonah setting up camp in his shelter above Nineveh would have been especially significant to the original reader. The word "shelter" or "booth" in verse 5 is intentionally chosen by the writer. It is the Hebrew word *sukkah*, and its inclusion here deliberately calls to mind the Feast of Booths. This yearly festival, also called the Feast of Tabernacles or Sukkoth, was celebrated when the time came for harvesting olives and grapes. It was in part a celebration of God's provision of food for the year, but more importantly, it was a celebration of God's past and continued grace. During this festival, all Israelites were to build *sukkahs*, or booths, and live in them for seven days in remembrance of when they lived in tents in the wilderness after God delivered them from slavery in Egypt. This feast was a joyful celebration of God's salvation, a time of remembering how He provided food and water even though they grumbled against Him and how He went with them and dwelled in a tabernacle among them even though they rebelled against Him and worshiped idols.

As Jonah sets up his own *sukkah*, he ironically embodies the opposite of what this festival represents. The Feast of Booths called the Israelites to rejoice in the God who is "a compassionate and gracious God, slow to anger and abounding in faithful love and truth, maintaining faithful love to a thousand generations, forgiving iniquity, rebellion, and sin" (Exodus 34:6-7), but instead, Jonah burns with anger that those things are true of the Lord. The Feast of Booths was a celebration in which even Gentiles were invited to take part (Deuteronomy 16:14), but Jonah wants deliverance only for his own people. As Jonah sits in his booth, he desires not mercy but destruction.

True love for God results in love for others, and Jonah's anger and lack of compassion illustrate the outcome of a heart that does not love the Lord. God's character is good and holy and something that should be a source of delight, but Jonah despises the Lord's compassion as evil. The problem is not first and foremost that Jonah does not have compassion for the Ninevites but that he lacks a love for who God is. Those who love the Lord delight in the things that He delights in, but Jonah is disgusted by them. God does not "take any pleasure in the death of the wicked" (Ezekiel 18:23). Rather God takes "pleasure when he turns from his ways and lives" (Ezekiel 18:23). Jonah's desires do not reflect the heart of the Lord, but instead he takes pleasure in the Ninevites death and is outraged by their repentance that leads to life.

Love for God is something that only He can supply, and so we must come humbly to Him, asking that He would produce that love in us. We can only have genuine love for the Lord and for others when we have first experienced His love for us. "We love because He first loved us" (1 John 4:19). And so, we come to Him in prayer, knowing those who earnestly seek Him will find Him (Deuteronomy 4:29, Jeremiah 29:13, Matthew 7:7), asking Him to fill us with His fullness so that we can know the depths of His love (Ephesians 3:14-19). We come to His Word, remembering His faithfulness and trusting that He will be good now, even when we do not see it. May we set up booths in our hearts, not to wish evil on others but to rejoice in the character of our compassionate God.

———— " ————

Those who love the Lord delight in the things that He delights in.

QUESTIONS

How does understanding the historical context of the Feast of Booths enhance your understanding of Jonah 4:5?

_____

_____

_____

_____

_____

_____

Read 1 John 4:7-11. What does this passage reveal about the relationship between loving God and loving others?

_____

_____

_____

_____

_____

_____

Where do you see a lack of love and compassion for others in your own heart?
Write a prayer confessing these things and asking God to produce His love in you.

_____

_____

_____

_____

_____

_____

GOD IS CALLING THE WAYWARD PROPHET BACK TO HIMSELF.

A MERCIFUL LESSON FROM A MERCIFUL GOD

Read Jonah 4:5-11

In the final verses of the book of Jonah, God gives a poignant lesson on His character and our response to it. Jonah has set up his booth, hopeful that he will witness the destruction of Nineveh. Evidently, his make-shift shelter is insufficient to protect him from the heat, so God causes a plant to grow over Jonah to give him shade to save him from his discomfort. The plant is a gift of compassion from the Lord. Jonah was greatly pleased by the plant, a grammatical construction that mirrors Jonah 4:1 when he was greatly displeased over Nineveh's repentance and God's merciful response. This parallelism emphasizes the hypocritical contrast between Jonah's joy and gratitude for his own salvation and his anger over the salvation of the Ninevites.

The narrator again emphasizes God's sovereignty over His creation through repetition of the word translated "appoint." Just as God appointed the fish to swallow Jonah, He now appoints the plant, the worm, and the scorching east wind. God sends a worm to eat away at the plant so that it withers and dies. He also appoints a wind that brings with it unbearable, scorching heat, which Jonah is now defenseless against. God is working in all that He ordains to reveal Himself and sanctify Jonah. God is using both comfort and discomfort to refine Jonah. All of these things are instruments of God's compassion, because in them, God is calling the wayward prophet back to Himself.

Jonah finds himself tormented by the heat and once again proclaims that he would rather die than go on living. At this point, God repeats His earlier question by asking Jonah if it is right for him to be angry. This time, Jonah exclaims that he is right to be angry. Like an enraged child who erupts at his parent's chastisement, Jonah's hot anger boils over as God deals out the final straw. Jonah's anger has been building because of God's mercy toward the Gentiles, but Jonah has failed to realize that he, like the Ninevites, is equally undeserving of God's compassion. His false sense of entitlement carries over into his anger at God for taking away the plant, and instead of recognizing that every good thing is a gift from God and that even the plant was an unmerited gift of grace, He is angry when it is gone.

God's response to Jonah in verses 10 and 11 is a powerfully humbling statement in the midst of Jonah's tantrum of rage. God shows Jonah his own disordered values by comparing his care for the plant to his lack of concern for a city full of people. Throughout the narrative, Jonah has been resistant to the potential loss of human life, both that of the mariners and of the Ninevites, and now the first time that he shows any kind of concern for something perishing is toward a plant. Jonah is concerned for his own comfort but not for the lives of the Ninevites. He pities a plant, but he has no compassion for the 120,000 souls who bear God's image.

God's final words in the book of Jonah emphasize the tender nature of His compassion for those whom He has created. God describes the Ninevites as not knowing their right hand from their left, a Hebrew idiom that indicates sinners are unable to discern right from wrong. God's attitude toward the sinful Ninevites is like that of Jesus in Matthew 9:36 when he looks out upon the crowds of people and has compassion on them because they are "distressed and dejected, like sheep without a shepherd." The people in the crowds, as well as the Ninevites, are a product of their own sin and fallen nature, and they deserve judgment, but God looks on them with compassion, and He has done the same for us. But what about us? When we see our neighbors living in sin, do we look on them with compassion or with hatred? When we see a world filled with wickedness and unrighteousness, do we look upon it with love or arrogant judgment. Let us not forget that God rescued us from the pit of our sin, and yet He showed us compassion.

God is a compassionate God, and the book of Jonah poignantly displays His tender mercy and loving-kindness to sinners. Time and time again, God is merciful when He does not have to be. God could have let the pagan sailors continue in their worship of false gods and left them to die in the sea, but He rescued them from idolatry and death. God could have left the Ninevites in their wickedness and rained His judgment upon them, but He gave them the gift of repentance and life. God could have left Jonah to the consequences of His own disobedience, but He graciously rescued him and revealed Himself to him even through trials.

The story ends abruptly with a question left unanswered, and we are invited to answer it ourselves. Will we see the beauty of the God who shows mercy to sinners? Will we recognize the extravagant grace that God has shown to us? Will we extend compassion to His image bearers in need of the Good Shepherd? May we return to Him, and may our hearts rejoice in the merciful, gracious, steadfast love of the Lord.

"...RETURN TO THE LORD YOUR GOD. FOR HE IS GRACIOUS AND COMPASSIONATE, SLOW TO ANGER, ABOUNDING IN FAITHFUL LOVE, AND HE RELENTS FROM SENDING DISASTER."

JOEL 2:13

QUESTIONS

How does the language of today's passage reveal the state of Jonah's heart? How do you see yourself in Jonah?

_____

_____

_____

_____

_____

_____

What does today's passage reveal about God's character? How is it similar or different from how you think about God?

_____

_____

_____

_____

_____

_____

How would you honestly answer God's final question to Jonah? Write a prayer asking God to help you to rejoice in His compassion and extend it to others.

_____

_____

_____

_____

_____

_____

MAY JONAH POINT OUR
HEARTS TO JESUS.

SOMETHING BETTER THAN JONAH

Read Matthew 12:38-41

All of Scripture points to Jesus. The deepest longings of our hearts and every promise of God find their fulfillment in Christ. We may be tempted to think that Jesus is only in the New Testament, but when we read the Bible with eyes to find Him, we will see Him from beginning to end. Every flawed would-be hero points to the perfect hero to come. Every gift of God's mercy sings of the One whose death makes mercy possible. Every bit of this big story is heading toward its glorious end in Jesus Christ.

In Matthew 12, Jesus makes a connection between the wayward prophet, Jonah, to Himself, the true Prophet. As the Pharisees stand before the One whom all the Scriptures have been anticipating, they ask for a sign. They do not want Jesus; they want someone else. Jesus tells them that the only sign they will receive is the sign of Jonah — Jonah's three day and three night stay in the belly of the fish points to Jesus's three day and three night stay in the heart of the earth. Jonah anticipates the Messiah who would die and be raised three days later. As Jesus tells the Pharisees, something better than Jonah is here.

God called Jonah to leave the comfort of his home to bring God's Word to an undeserving people who were far from Him, but Jonah refused. God asked His Son to leave heaven, His throne, His glory, and His comfort to undergo excruciating suffering and death for an undeserving people who were His enemies, and Jesus willingly agreed.

Jonah fled from God's will, believing that obedience would mean pain. Jesus, fully aware of the unspeakable suffering He would experience as the fullness of God's wrath was poured out upon Him, cried out through sweat like drops of blood, "Not my will, but yours, be done" (Luke 22:42-44).

Jonah did everything He could to avoid bringing a message of mercy to sinners, but Jesus went to great lengths, even to death, to pursue us while we were in the depths of sin, like a shepherd who leaves the ninety-nine to rescue his one lost sheep (Romans 5:8, Matthew 18:12).

Jonah's sin brings the storm of God's judgment, putting others in harm's way. Jesus calms the storm and saves the sinners on the boat. Jonah was helpless against the torrents of the sea. Jesus is sovereign over the winds and the waves because He is God.

Jonah cried out from the heart of the seas, "I am driven from your sight!" But God's presence never left him. Jesus cried out from the cross, "My God, my God, why have you forsaken me?" as He experienced the hell of separation from God so that we might draw near to His presence (Matthew 27:46).

Jonah received the Word of God as His prophet and reluctantly delivered it to sinners. Jesus is the Word who willingly became flesh and who has the words of eternal life to save sinners (John 1:14, John 6:68).

Jonah would rather die than see the Ninevites receive mercy. Jesus died so that we could be shown mercy.

Something better than Jonah is indeed here. As we feel the conviction of our own hard hearts reflected in Jonah, may we look to the One whose compassion for us abounds. As we mourn that Jonah, like so many of us, was reluctant to share the grace that he had been given, let us rejoice that Christ is the longed-for prophet who willingly gave Himself to offer us grace. May we not see the book of Jonah as merely a moral lesson that we must follow but as a vibrant picture of the compassionate heart of God that compels us to extend that same compassion to others, not to earn His grace but because He has lavished His grace on us. May Jonah point our hearts to Jesus.

"

The deepest longings of our hearts and every promise of God find their fulfillment in Christ.

QUESTIONS

What was your perspective on the book of Jonah before beginning this study? How has your understanding of this book changed?

_____

_____

_____

_____

_____

_____

_____

How does the book of Jonah deepen your understanding of the gospel?

_____

_____

_____

_____

_____

_____

_____

As you reflect back over the book of Jonah as a whole, what has God revealed to you through His Word about who He is? How should that change the way you live?

_____

_____

_____

_____

_____

_____

_____

Those who cherish
worthless idols abandon
their faithful love, but as
for me, I will sacrifice to you
with a voice of thanksgiving.
I will fulfill what I have vowed.
Salvation belongs to the Lord.

JONAH 2:8-9

WEEK FOUR REFLECTION

REVIEW JONAH 3:5 - 4:11

Paraphrase the passage from this week.

_____

_____

_____

_____

_____

_____

_____

_____

_____

What did you observe from this week's text about God and His character?

_____

_____

_____

_____

_____

_____

_____

_____

_____

What does this week's passage reveal about the condition of mankind and yourself?

_____

_____

_____

_____

_____

_____

_____

_____

_____

How does this passage point to the gospel?

_____

_____

_____

_____

_____

How should you respond to this passage? What specific action steps can you take this week to apply this passage?

_____

_____

_____

_____

_____

Write a prayer in response to your study of God's Word. Adore God for who He is, confess sins that He revealed in your own life, ask Him to empower you to walk in obedience, and pray for anyone who comes to mind as you study.

LITERARY DEVICES IN THE BOOK OF JONAH

CHIASM/CHIASTIC STRUCTURE

A literary structure in which a progression of ideas is paralleled in reverse order.

EUPHEMISM

A word or expression used to replace another idea that may be considered harsh or more intense.

- *Using the word "down" as a euphemism for death in Jonah 1 and 2.*

FORESHADOWING

An indication of something that is to come.

- *Possible foreshadowing of Nineveh's repentance with the double meaning of "overthrown" or "demolished" in Jonah 3:4.*

HYPERBOLE

Exaggeration for the sake of emphasis.

- *"I cried out for help from deep inside Sheol." Jonah 2:2*

IMAGERY

The use of figurative or descriptive language that appeals to the senses.

- *"The water engulfed me up to the neck; the watery depths overcame me; seaweed was wrapped around my head." Jonah 2:5*

IRONY

Intentional disruption of the reader's expectation through language that carries a different meaning than is to be expected or through events that do not correspond with what the reader expects to happen.

- *The pagan sailors calling on Jonah, the prophet, to pray in Jonah 2.*
- *The Ninevites' humble repentance in contrast to Jonah's prideful rebellion in Jonah 3.*
- *Jonah's joy over his own salvation and anger over Nineveh's salvation in Jonah 4.*

MERISM

When two extremes represent the whole.

- *God making "the sea and the dry land" in Jonah 1:9 indicates that He made everything.*

PARALLELISM

Recurrence of a grammatical structure or pattern within a sentence.

- *"I called out to the Lord in my distress, and he answered me. I cried out for help from deep inside Sheol; you heard my voice." Jonah 2:1*

PERSONIFICATION

Giving a non-human thing human characteristics.

- *The ship threatening to break apart (Jonah 1:4)*
- *The belly of Sheol (Jonah 2:2)*

REPETITION

Recurrence of a word, phrase, or idea for emphasis or to communicate a particular meaning.

- *Down (Jonah 1-2)*

SYNTAX

The intentional structuring of a sentence to emphasize a particular word or words, most often by placing a word at the beginning or end of a sentence.

- *"The Lord" in Jonah 1:9 is written first in the Hebrew syntax to emphasize the importance of Yahweh as the one true God.*
- *"Believed" in Johan 3:5 is written first in the Hebrew syntax to emphasize the immediacy of the Ninevites' belief.*

JONAH & JESUS

JONAH	JESUS
"The word of the Lord came to Jonah son of Amittai" JONAH 1:1	"The Word became flesh and dwelt among us. We observed his glory, the glory as the one and only Son from the Father, full of grace and truth." JOHN 1:14
"Jonah got up to flee to Tarshish from the Lord's presence. He went down to Joppa and found a ship going to Tarshish. He paid the fare and went down into it to go with them to Tarshish from the Lord's presence." JONAH 1:3	"he humbled himself by becoming obedient to the point of death—even to death on a cross." PHILIPPIANS 2:8 "My Father, if it is possible, let this cup pass from me. Yet not as I will, but as you will." MATTHEW 26:39
"The captain approached him and said, 'What are you doing sound asleep? Get up! Call to your god. Maybe this god will consider us, and we won't perish.'" JONAH 1:6	"He was in the stern, sleeping on the cushion. So they woke him up and said to him, 'Teacher! Don't you care that we're going to die?' He got up, rebuked the wind, and said to the sea, 'Silence! Be still!' The wind ceased, and there was a great calm." MARK 4:38-39
"Then they picked up Jonah and threw him into the sea, and the sea stopped its raging." JONAH 1:15	"By this will, we have been sanctified through the ottering of the body of Jesus Christ once for all time." HEBREWS 10:10

JONAH	JESUS
"The Lord appointed a great fish to swallow Jonah, and Jonah was in the belly of the fish three days and three nights." JONAH 1:17	"For as Jonah was in the belly of the huge fish three days and three nights, so the Son of Man will be in the heart of the earth three days and three nights." MATTHEW 12:40
"But I said, 'I have been banished from your sight'" JONAH 2:4A	"About three in the afternoon Jesus cried out with a loud voice, 'Eli, Eli, lema sabachthani?' that is, 'My God, my God, why have you abandoned me?'" MATTHEW 27:46
"God saw their actions—that they had turned from their evil ways—so God relented from the disaster he had threatened them with. And he did not do it. Jonah was greatly displeased and became furious." JONAH 3:10-4:1	"I tell you, in the same way, there will be more joy in heaven over one sinner who repents than over ninety-nine righteous people who don't need repentance." LUKE 15:7
"And now, Lord, take my life from me, for it is better for me to die than to live." JONAH 4:3	"But God proves his own love for us in that while we were still sinners, Christ died for us." ROMANS 5:8

What is the Gospel?

THANK YOU FOR READING AND ENJOYING THIS STUDY WITH US! WE ARE ABUNDANTLY GRATEFUL FOR THE WORD OF GOD, THE INSTRUCTION WE GLEAN FROM IT, AND THE EVER-GROWING UNDERSTANDING IT PROVIDES FOR US OF GOD'S CHARACTER. WE ARE ALSO THANKFUL THAT SCRIPTURE CONTINUALLY POINTS TO ONE THING IN INNUMERABLE WAYS: THE GOSPEL.

We remember our brokenness when we read about the fall of Adam and Eve in the garden of Eden (Genesis 3), where sin entered into a perfect world and maimed it. We remember the necessity that something innocent must die to pay for our sin when we read about the atoning sacrifices in the Old Testament. We read that we have all sinned and fallen short of the glory of God (Romans 3:23) and that the penalty for our brokenness, the wages of our sin, is death (Romans 6:23). We all need grace and mercy, but most importantly, we all need a Savior.

We consider the goodness of God when we realize that He did not plan to leave us in this dire state. We see His promise to buy us back from the clutches of sin and death in Genesis 3:15. And we see that promise accomplished with Jesus Christ on the cross. Jesus Christ knew no sin yet became sin so that we might become righteous through His sacrifice (2 Corinthians 5:21). Jesus was tempted in every way that we are and lived sinlessly. He was reviled yet still yielded Himself for our sake, that we may have life abundant in Him. Jesus lived the perfect life that we could not live and died the death that we deserved.

The gospel is profound yet simple. There are many mysteries in it that we will never understand this side of heaven, but there is still overwhelming weight to its implications in this life. The gospel tells of our sinfulness and God's goodness and a gracious gift that compels a response. We are saved by grace through faith, which means that we rest with faith in the grace that Jesus Christ displayed on the cross (Ephesians 2:8-9). We cannot save ourselves from our brokenness or do any amount of good works to merit God's favor. Still, we can have faith that what Jesus accomplished in His death, burial, and resurrection was more than enough for our salvation and our eternal delight. When we accept God, we are commanded to die to ourselves and our sinful desires and live a life worthy of the calling we have received (Ephesians 4:1). The gospel compels us to be sanctified, and in so doing, we are conformed to the likeness of Christ Himself. This is hope. This is redemption. This is the gospel.

SCRIPTURES TO REFERENCE:

GENESIS 3:15
I will put hostility between you and the woman, and between your offspring and her offspring. He will strike your head, and you will strike his heel.

ROMANS 3:23
For all have sinned and fall short of the glory of God.

ROMANS 6:23
For the wages of sin is death, but the gift of God is eternal life in Christ Jesus our Lord.

2 CORINTHIANS 5:21
He made the one who did not know sin to be sin for us, so that in him we might become the righteousness of God.

EPHESIANS 2:8-9
For you are saved by grace through faith, and this is not from yourselves; it is God's gift — not from works, so that no one can boast.

EPHESIANS 4:1-3
Therefore I, the prisoner in the Lord, urge you to walk worthy of the calling you have received, with all humility and gentleness, with patience, bearing with one another in love, making every effort to keep the unity of the Spirit through the bond of peace.

Thank You

for studying God's Word with us

CONNECT WITH US

@THEDAILYGRACECO
@DAILYGRACEPODCAST

CONTACT US

INFO@THEDAILYGRACECO.COM

SHARE

#THEDAILYGRACECO

VISIT US ONLINE

WWW.THEDAILYGRACECO.COM

MORE DAILY GRACE

DAILY GRACE® PODCAST